Surviving the Twenty-First Century

Essays from Montaigbakhtinian.com

By William Eaton

Surviving the Twenty-First Century

Essays from Montaigbakhtinian.com

By William Eaton

Serving House Books

Surviving the Twenty-First Century

ISBN: 978-0-9862146-3-9

Cover photograph: Anne Fassotte

Author photograph: Sarah Shatz

Section art: Richard Delgado

Serving House Books logo by Barry Lereng Wilmont

Published by Serving House Books
Copenhagen, Denmark and Florham Park, NJ
www.servinghousebooks.com

Member of The Independent Book Publishers Association

First Serving House Books Edition 2015

Note: *A version of "Wild life, wild mind" was published in 2013 in* The Chronicle of Higher Education, *and "Sick" appeared in the Web del Sol* Choices *e-chapbook. These publishers are thanked for allowing these pieces to reappear in the present collection.*

Thanks to Molly Renda for design consultation.

Contents

7   Introduction & Acknowledgements

Getting Our Feet Wet
11   Story of New York
12   Where are our dreams?
17   Wild life, wild mind
21   On starting over

On Beyond Courtesy
25   The palest of intimacies
27   Of courtesy
29   I was waiting to use the bathroom
31   Warmth's truth
38   It was a warm, sunny day
41   Zeroing in

The Practice of Philosophy
47   On just being
53   The practice of philosophy
62   In winter
64   On just playing

Stealin', Stealin'
73   Stealin', Stealin'
80   Sick
85   Ethics of our twenty-first century
95   My bar mitzvah (and Thanksgiving) speech

What Shall I Learn of Parenting or Parenting of Me?
111   Of wonders still
114   What shall I learn of parenting or parenting of me?
122   Nurture
128   The connection between shoe-tying and world peace

Introduction & Acknowledgments

Enough is enough. I would let readers pass quickly to the essays themselves, dipping and skipping as they may.

With one exception drafts of the essays contained in this volume appeared on my blog, Montaigbakhtinian.com. It is hoped that by uniting them in a single collection, readers will find connections, and new wonderings, that were not apparent in the original, drafting stage.

Allow me to offer tremendous thanks to three people. Walter Cummins had the idea for this collection and has overseen its development. It would not exist without him. Fourteen years ago Anne got me launched, or I her, on the adventure of parenting, which has played such a large and wonderful (and at times heart-breaking) role in my life and in these essays. They would not exist without her.

As for Jonah, our son, and the Sancho Panza of the present collection, no kind words can equal the warmth and companionship he has brought to my life. There should be a god, a great god, to thank for allowing me to share years of my life with such a boy.

— Wm. Eaton
Lisbon, Portugal

Getting Our Feet Wet

The Great Society is a place where every child can find knowledge to enrich his mind and to enlarge his talents. It is a place where leisure is a welcome chance to build and reflect, not a feared cause of boredom and restlessness. It is a place where the city of man serves not only the needs of the body and the demands of commerce but the desire for beauty and the hunger for community. It is a place where man can renew contact with nature. It is a place which honors creation for its own sake and for what it adds to the understanding of the race. It is a place where men are more concerned with the quality of their goals than the quantity of their goods.

—Lyndon Baines Johnson, "Great Society" speech, given at
the University of Michigan in Ann Arbor, May 22, 1964.

Story of New York

A Thanksgiving Day several years ago, my son Jonah and I had been ice skating at the rink in Central Park and were walking to Lincoln Center to see a performance of the Big Apple Circus. Jonah (8 at the time) was hungry and proposed that I buy him a hot dog from a street vendor. As I was not in the habit of doing this, I was not sure how much the hot dog cost. The vendor's cart was missing a price list. I took out three dollars and offered it to the man, asking if this was right. With a quick nod he took the money.

Later I saw another such vendor's cart on which the price was clearly posted: $2. I said to Jonah, "That guy cheated me out of a dollar."

"Yes," Jonah said, with a tone that implied that he had known the correct price all along. "But he needed that dollar more than you."

Somewhat later, after the show, we were almost home, walking through our park-like real-estate development, a tree-lined battleground, capital and real-estate interests on one side, wage-dependent tenants on the other, and lawyers and politicians somewhere in between. I came back to the subject of the hot dog. "The dollar isn't the issue. It's the cheating. It's the effect that it has on you, on your relations with people, to feel that everyone— the hot dog sellers, the taxi drivers, the credit-card companies and investment bankers, your landlord—everyone is ready to cheat you, is looking for opportunities to cheat you, to take advantage of your paying attention to anything besides money. To your paying attention to your son, for example—to enjoying your son's company. It's as if we're surrounded by people who are only interested in money."

"Papa," Jonah said patiently, "what do you think people come to New York for?"

Where are our dreams?

Five notes stemming from the collapse of the Soviet Union

1   In June 2012 Jonah and I spent ten days in Moscow and visiting Yasnaya Polyana, Tolstoy's estate about one hundred miles to the south. On the last night of our trip, Ludmila, the woman with whom we were staying, made dinner, and, as usual, Jonah slipped away after eating to go in our room and listen to his iTunes and communicate with his friends in the West via Google+. In the kitchen, Ludmila and I talked in Russian while she washed the dishes. I had just read an article about a piece of Russian history that never ceases to be discussed: the killing of the Tsar and his family by the Bolsheviks. Ludmila commented that this had been horrible, and I agreed. However, I said, if I had been one of the Bolsheviks I would have done the same thing. The existence of the Tsar and his family was a flame keeping alive the hopes of reactionaries and members of the upper classes more generally, and thereby fanning the flames of the civil war then raging. And it was hardly as if the Tsar's forces and those of his predecessors had not killed many of their opponents, to say nothing of the millions of Russians killed in the First World War—killed while trying to defend, being forced to defend, the Tsar's kingdom. Ludmila then said that the fact was that человечество—humanity—was horrible and that it was hard not to think that the world would be a better, more peaceful place without the human race.

2   I first visited Moscow in 1969. In the 1990s, in the aftermath of perestroika, Jonah, his mother and I had gone many times to St. Petersburg, lived there for months at a time. But it had been years since we'd been back, more years since we'd been in Moscow. And, as people had warned me in advance, the Moscow region was now extraordinarily similar to the United States we knew: awash

in automobiles, cellphones, consumerism. A prevalence of washing machines and perhaps dietary changes (less pork) had taken away the particular smell I associated with Russia. The elaborate, annoying, bureaucratic, absurd visa procedures remained, but now the US government had adopted similar procedures. Among the differences I was left to remark on were the summer dresses of young middle-class Moscow women, which dresses seemed, in their simple way, to render their wearers more attractive than the not-all-that-different clothing of young women in Western Europe and New York. If any evidence remained of the famous Russian soul, it was Tolstoy's tomb, a grass-covered rectangular mound about six feet long at the edge of the woods.

A feeling to 2012 Moscow caused me to recall Camus' description of Oran, Algeria, at the beginning of *La peste*:

> Of course nothing is more natural these days than to see people working from day until night and then choosing to lose—playing games or in a cafe, chatting—the rest of their waking hours. But there are cities and countries where people have, from time to time, an intimation that there might be something else [to existence]. . . . Oran, by contrast, seems a city without intimations; in other words, it is a completely modern city.

3 Ludmila's comment about человечество was the most original, traditionally Russian and un-modern moment of Jonah and my ten days in Moscow, and it might be said that it was largely because of my appreciation of such comments, of the alternative perspective they continued to offer me, that I had spent years of my life trying to learn Russian and braving the visa bureaucracy so that I might spend time in the country. Among the differences I had been introduced to along the way—and first in a trip to Stalingrad when I was 14 years old—was the perspective of a people who over many centuries had been invaded by any number of avaricious, pitiless hordes (Napoleon's army, two waves of the German army and Western capitalism being only the latest of them). Enslaved, tortured, worked to death by their own leaders as well, Russians

feel viscerally the lack of geographical, institutional or cultural barriers to protect them from future disaster.

It was in this context that I interpreted Ludmila's comment. In the United States we take new cars and electronic devices and the attractiveness of young women, and of young men, as positive signs, as signs of economic and physical health, and thus of health *tout court*. But for Ludmila this was not enough. In such superficial acquisitions and appearances there was nothing on which one might pin hopes for a future notably different from the past. By contrast, the Soviet communists, for all their shortcomings, had championed a humanitarian ideal: of putting community before self-interest, of sharing rather than exploiting. "From each according to his ability, to each according to his need."

In intellectual circles a distinction is made between "negative rights" (civil and political rights, things like freedom of speech and assembly, freedom from slavery, the right to a fair trial, laws enshrining and protecting private property) and "positive rights" (economic, social and cultural rights, things like freedom from hunger and cold; government-supplied education, health care, pensions, police protection, maternity leave). From this perspective, one of the major intended or unintended consequences of the West's winning the Cold War is that it has come to be accepted worldwide that negative rights are fundamental to a healthy, sustainable state, and that positive rights are a luxury which rich states might or might not choose to provide to the wage-and-fee-dependent (who include, among many others, house cleaners, waiters, store clerks, teachers and professors, accountants, doctors and lawyers).

4   One might decide that an alternative, the Soviet approach or another more cooperative approach, was not given a sufficient test. One might decide that the Soviet approach was discredited and dismissed not so much on account of its shortcomings as by external enemies or on account of the financing on which the experiment depended: the value in global, capitalist markets of Russia's vast natural resources. (And thus the precipitous rise in global oil prices during the 1970s generated expectations that could not be

sustained when these prices receded in the 1980s.) Or one might decide that the Soviet experiment had proved a failure. But in either case, what after the collapse of the Soviet Union is left? SUVs, washing machines, iTunes, pretty summer dresses? Do we retain any intimations that—in addition to our products and our periodic political, financial and environmental catastrophes—there might be something else?

> Our fellow citizens [in Oran] work long hours, but always to get more money. Business is what interests them above all; making money is what they believe they were made to do. Of course they also enjoy simple pleasures—coupling up, going to the movies, bathing in the Mediterranean. But, judiciously, they reserve such pleasures for Saturday evenings and Sundays, trying, the rest of the week, to earn a lot of money.

Washing dishes in the kitchen of her fourth-floor apartment in one of Moscow's kilometers upon kilometers of housing projects, Ludmila said that now everyone—человечество—is just waiting for the next catastrophe. World war, government upheaval, environmental disaster. New York under water as a result of global warming—that was one of the possibilities she mentioned. And if we have lost our faith in humanity, she said, if we have lost the hope that human beings might be able to work together for their own mutual benefit, and aspire to something larger than a car, something more nourishing than the latest gadgets and fashions—then what faith, what hope do we have? And how, this was her question, how can people live without hope?

5   I have long had in mind to write something about Lyndon Johnson's great "Great Society" speech, given at the University of Michigan in 1964. I take this speech, like the Civil Rights Movement, the space race and some of our more humane occupational safety and health regulations, to be a product of the existence of the Soviet Union, of the pressure that competition with the Soviet

Union put on the United States and its citizens to strive to reach higher goals. "The purpose of protecting the life of our nation and preserving the liberty of our citizens is to pursue the happiness of our people. Our success in that pursuit is the test of our success as a nation," LBJ said.

> The challenge of the next half century is whether we have the wisdom to use that wealth to enrich and elevate our national life, and to advance the quality of our American civilization. . . . The Great Society rests on abundance and liberty for all. It demands an end to poverty and racial injustice, to which we are totally committed in our time. But that is just the beginning. The Great Society is a place where every child can find knowledge to enrich his mind and to enlarge his talents. It is a place where leisure is a welcome chance to build and reflect, not a feared cause of boredom and restlessness. It is a place where the city of man serves not only the needs of the body and the demands of commerce but the desire for beauty and the hunger for community. It is a place where man can renew contact with nature. It is a place which honors creation for its own sake and for what it adds to the understanding of the race. It is a place where men are more concerned with the quality of their goals than the quantity of their goods.

LBJ's next half century is now over. Where are our dreams?

3

Wild life, wild mind

None of us can ever retrieve that innocence before all theory.
— Susan Sontag, "Against Interpretation"

There is that moment, which usually seems quite unremarkable, when we realize that we are having fun or that we are deeply engaged in some activity—dancing, talking with a friend, clipping toenails, what have you. What is not only interesting about the moment, but also sad, is that it usually marks the end of that particular pleasure. We may continue to dance, converse, or preen, but it will now be a more complex experience, in which the fun is mixed with something else—the consciousness of having fun, or of being engaged.

One gentle summer day, Jonah, one of his cousins and I rented kayaks and headed out on a mountain lake in Vermont. No one else was in sight, and we were neither under a flight path nor within earshot of a highway. We pulled up in a cove, and Jonah got us happily engaged slinging handfuls of muddy clay and clumps of water grass at one another.

After a while, I left the boys to continue the laughing battle on their own, and I lay down in the reeds across the way. Quickly I was surrounded by little snails and insects of various sizes. A few of these smaller animals found their ways onto my arms and legs and began hunting for food. The pleasure of this, for me, may have had something to do with my not being a scientist, that is, with my not feeling the need to observe these creatures closely. I was glad to share with them a bit of myself and the afternoon.

It was around one o'clock, more than six hours of daylight remaining. The thought came to me that this was turning out to be one of the most wonderful days of my life. I thought that after lunch the boys and I might move on to another part of the lake, and I might lounge among a different grouping of plants and animals. But by recognizing my feeling of well-being, I put an end to it.

Later that day I was reading a chapter about Susan Sontag in Daniel Horowitz's *Consuming Pleasures*. The chapter contained these lines from Sontag's essay "Against Interpretation":

> In a culture whose already classical dilemma is the hypertrophy of the intellect at the expense of energy and sensual capability, interpretation is the revenge of the intellect upon art.

> Even more. It is the revenge of the intellect upon the world. To interpret is to impoverish, to deplete the world—in order to set up a shadow world of "meanings."

While noting that Sontag was, as I am, an inveterate assigner of meanings (that is, interpretations), I might propose that interpretation, essay writing included, is also the revenge of the intellect upon experience. That doesn't seem quite right though. For one, interpreting, theorizing, ruminating, wishing, regretting, getting revenge, writing, reading, quoting: all this, too, is experience, being part of the world and absorbed in it.

I wonder also about the "revenge" in Sontag's assertion. It implies a conflict, which certainly is there, between mediated and unmediated experience. It also raises this question: What would experience (or art) do to the intellect that would make it want to fight back? Sontag writes that "real art"—and real nature and real experience, I would add—"has the capacity to make us nervous. By reducing the work of art to its content and then interpreting that, one tames the work of art. Interpretation makes art manageable, conformable."

And so we might imagine that lurking in the reeds beside me was the possibility of reconnection to my animal nature, to my carnality, and to a world not unlike the world of business in which there is nothing remarkable about being simultaneously predator and prey. Or would the nervousness come from lying in warm water—reminders of my very first months in my mother's womb? Sontag singled out Kafka and Beckett as two artists whose work had been besieged by interpretations. We might say then that "real art" makes us nervous because of how it bypasses thought processes and categories, finding a home in our unconscious, in the wilderness of our minds.

Heading in the other direction, in *La pensée sauvage,* Lévi-Strauss proposes that we have been driven to develop conscious processes and classification systems, and to science, by the chaos of our sensations and of the world outside of science. Sontag urges us to "recover our senses. We must learn to see more, to hear more, to feel more." But Lévi-Strauss seems to be saying that life—and, I will now add, art that moves us—routinely gives us more than we can handle without intellectual defenses.

After Jonah, Karim and I left the lake and drove back to our B&B, they returned to their fantasy novels and electronic games. All I had left were memories and thoughts, and my capacity to hold on to them with prose. The idea came to me that our interpretations are like hawsers, allowing us to drift away from our sensations—from what we experience, and all the feelings that our experiences provoke—while also keeping us connected. And inversely: We would so like to merge with others and with nature, to just be part of the chemistry; but with weapons like interpretation we do battle with our erotic urges, fighting to preserve our autonomy, to be able to join the games of life "without being threatened by a physical orgasm of local excitement," as the psychoanalyst D.W. Winnicott once put it.

We ignore how our thinking—about feelings, bodily functions, friends, politics, what's on the television—lets us down. I am not talking about the possibility that someone else—Sontag, say—might be smarter than I am or have more-incisive insights than I do. I am talking about thinking on a much more basic level: that a particular peach tastes particularly good, or wondering in the middle of kissing if it is going to lead to sex, or what's for dinner? This is hardly the same as tasting the peach or kissing.

All our lives include moments when we are nowhere—not coming or going; not judging or interpreting; sensing but not perceiving. At such moments we may be, Buddhist-style, absorbed in a Oneness of the universe. We may also be in touch with the multiplicities of the moment—with snails, insects, and shouting boys.

4

On starting over

1   Driving a friend's car, turn on the radio, NPR, I think. An actress is talking up a play she is in. Once a big name in Hollywood, now she is doing Brecht at a regional theater. She knows the talk, though, the promotional talk. She says that now, having gotten older and wiser, she is only interested in roles she could fail in. If success is guaranteed, she says, there's no learning. (I remember once talking with someone who studied child development in Africa. One of his principal messages was that stress was crucial to learning. In the absence of stress you don't learn.)

I think of "my" journal, *Zeteo*; this seems often a project that might fail, at which I might fail, and I can imagine that this is part of what makes it a good project. Perhaps not so much for the challenge of beating back failure as because life, too, is tenuous, and thus tenuousness can make one feel alive.

2   In Paris for several weeks, I have my annual dinner with a childhood friend, an American who came to Paris to live with her boyfriend. In fits and starts, over the course of half a dozen years, my friend has come to feel more and more at home in Paris, though she still has a ways to go and spends several months each year back in the United States. I ask her what steps one would take, as an American, to make a life for oneself in Paris.

Before she has a chance to answer, I note my family's standard approach: do research, make a list, every week try to do a few things in order to meet people, find one's society. That's what I should have done, my friend said, but I didn't. She likes to go hiking, but it took her three years to look up the French word for hiking in a dictionary, with an idea of finding people to go hiking with. For much of the first years she was lonely and uncomfortable, planning her trips back to the United States.

3   A year or so ago I was told a story about a woman in her sixties whose husband had died not long before. After some stretch of grieving, she was cleaning out the suburban house in which she and her husband had lived and raised a family. She was going to move to the big city. Although this city was not far from her suburban home, in my mind the widow knew no one in this city. She was starting over. The person who told me the story connected the move with a decision to live. If, nearing old age, her husband and children gone, this woman was not going to fade away, she had to start over.

4   In two years I will be retired from my paying job, no longer have an office I have to go to, hours I have to work. Two years after that Jonah will start college. I have thought of moving to Paris or to any number of cities in southern Europe or in Central or South America. Writing in a half-empty café in a not charming part of Paris, with a large, nondescript building across the street covered in scaffolding and plastic, being renovated, I am thinking of how hard (like rock, breaking rock) such a move would be. Not so much the work of trying to find a place for myself in some corner of Parisian society, nor the challenge of the dark, wet-cold winters, nor the challenge of packing up, dispensing with almost forty years of New York life. I am thinking of years of loneliness and of feeling that I did not quite belong. And it seems as if this struggle would be the principal reason to make the move.

5   I have heard that the pianist Vladimir Horowitz used to take his grand piano with him from international concert hall to international concert hall. We can see advantages—the familiarity, the likelihood that this was a wonderful piano. And Horowitz has been considered a great pianist. Another person, however, would have appreciated the challenges, the fun even, of confronting different instruments, producing different sounds from night to night. I can even imagine finding something in wrestling with a broken-down piano, seeing what kinds of music you might together make.

II

On Beyond Courtesy

And NUH is the letter I use to spell Nutches
Who live in small caves, known as Nitches, for hutches,
These Nutches have troubles, the biggest of which is
The fact there are many more Nutches than Nitches.
Each Nutch in a Nitch knows that some other Nutch
Would like to move into his Nitch very much.
So each Nutch in a Nitch has to watch that small Nitch
Or Nutches who haven't got Nitches will snitch.

—Dr. Seuss, *On Beyond Zebra!*

The palest of intimacies

Many heterosexual men, I assume, have fantasies that involve dispensing with the negotiations and preliminaries of civilized sexual conquest. Seeing an attractive woman—a waitress, perhaps, a woman at a conference, in a hotel—they may imagine walking up to her, telling her they want to have sex with her, and she says something on the lines of "Yes, sure, right now!"

In *The Unbearable Lightness of Being*, Milan Kundera offered his variation: the doctor who tells a series of women to take off all their clothes, and they do. It is also interesting to recall a corollary to this fantasy: the male worry that a woman who would so readily agree to have sex must either be a prostitute, mentally ill or substantially less attractive than she at first seemed.

For some years now, while waiting in check-out lines I have had what seems to be a related fantasy. It arises when I see a young, attractive, reasonably well-to-do woman ahead of me. I see her digging money out of her purse or pockets, and I imagine her coming up a little short. My fantasy kicks in—perhaps, flustered and chagrined, she is going to have to set one of her items aside.

In a squeamish version this item might be a box of tampons, but this is the first time this has occurred to me; I am more drawn to a small box of cookies, a piece of fruit. Which, it will turn out, the young woman does not have to forgo, because I proffer the sum she needs. And then—this is what provides the more acute pleasure—I do *not* walk out of the store with this woman, I do not propose a cup of coffee, etc. I keep my head bowed. Like a robot Good Samaritan, I sense the young woman's needs, provide what's needed, withdraw my hand.

Obviously this is not quite the "random act of kindness" still urged by bumperstickers in university towns and other places where the full compass of self-interest is aggressively overlooked. The recipient of my generosity has hardly been chosen at random—besides my erotic interest, there is the fact that she hardly needs the gift.

Perhaps she and I both, and separately, tremble ever so slightly and privately, sensing the actual target of my magnanimity—sex.

Her lips part. She begins thanking me.

I shake my head, not wishing to have the "simple generosity" of my gift sullied by the suggestion that I was expecting even this palest of intimacies.

Of courtesy

We might urge people to do unto others, or, per Kant, to act only in accord with a principle that they would at the same time will to be universal law, but we should be clear that behaving in such a manner is more likely to encourage others to behave otherwise—to act more selfishly. This is not to say there aren't some people who, for instance, if you are courteous to them, will be more inclined to be courteous to you—and many more will enjoy saying thank you. But there are certainly those—to include many who, like me, earn their living on the island of Manhattan—who, seeing you behave in such an obliging fashion, may take you for a fool or an unambitious no-account. They will take advantage of your courteousness, generosity, understanding, et al., as it suits their needs or whims.

This is not to say that one should never be courteous, for instance. One might be courteous simply for the pleasure being courteous brings—although one should keep in mind that this pleasure has a great deal to do with two extravagant fantasies. The first is that acting courteously promotes courtesy, that it promotes a "better"—more orderly, well-mannered—world. The second is that acting courteously shows the fundamental goodness of one's nature. As Kant pointed out, the person who finds pleasure or other reward in behaving in an exemplary manner—who, for example, acts honorably because he wishes to be honored—"deserves praise and encouragement, but not esteem," self-interest being at the source of his behavior.

One might also be courteous where it produces more practical positive reactions. For example, one might be courteous with those people who *do* respond courteously to courtesy, or with people, such as a boss, who will take such behavior as a sign of deference and who will rarely be disturbed to find underlings appearing inferior.

It should also be noted that, insofar as the recipient of one's courtesy has not asked for it, he may, and often with good reason, resent or be suspicious of it, wondering what may be requested in return. (I recall a Chris Rock joke to the effect that every time a man holds a door or does another little favor for a woman he is proposing that they have sex.) The recipients of courtesies (from men and women) may feel they have been committed to a deal without having had the chance to even review the terms. One may sense a courteous person fancying that—not that he would ever mention it, but in fact—he is entitled to something, to his "thank you" at the very least. If a recipient senses as well the pleasure that a courteous person has taken in a courteous gesture, the recipient might wish for rather more recognition of the essential contribution that a recipient makes to this other's person's happiness.

I was waiting to use the bathroom

I was waiting to use the bathroom in the basement of an old-fashioned New York coffee shop. I might have wasted several minutes of my one priceless life there; no one was in the bathroom, the lock was broken. But a dishwasher—a Mexican-American "illegal immigrant," I would guess; a man working long hours for less than the minimum wage, no benefits—happened to walk by, and without a word fetched a knife and slipped the lock for me.

Here was a man who owed me nothing and could hope to get nothing more than thanks from me. And I hadn't even asked him to help me. And thus I more fully appreciated that he did help, and I felt a warm feeling of community with this man who didn't even speak my language, nor I his. Here, I felt, was another person who reacted like me, who shared my idea—or feeling—as to how people should behave toward one another.

Later that same week I brought a box of Q-Tips to a drugstore counter, and instead of just ringing it up and taking my money, the clerk told me there was a larger box on sale for the same price. When I couldn't find the box on the shelf, she came around from behind the sales counter to find it for me. In fact, I would have been just as happy buying 100 Q-Tips for $1.99 as 350, but I understood that this woman didn't realize this—to her the much lower cost per item was significant, well worth the unwieldiness and obscenity of such a large box of Q-Tips.

I realized that she liked saving people money. Probably she felt better about herself on account of this deed, for securing an extra 250 Q-Tips for a stranger, and so we could say that she was getting rather more from the transaction than I was. But, in fact, in this particular instance, my reward was much greater. Because, between this clerk and the dishwasher, I had a sense that New York harbors a secret society of people—a society of which I counted myself a member—people who have an eye out for the needs of others, for

29

people who (outside their being people) mean nothing to them.

It is a very odd society, for one because I suspect that most every New Yorker feels that this is a very small society, and that he or she is one of its most worthy members. I also wonder if the desire—or need—to help strangers isn't related to a lack of kin or cohorts who one can or wishes to help. I wonder if helping strangers isn't at times a perverse manifestation of the human instinct to help one's family or tribe. (Rousseau speaks of philosophers who love the Tartars so as not to have to love their neighbors.)

I have elsewhere written about how some seemingly altruistic acts may be, rather, attempts to influence others' behavior or to establish one's moral superiority. There is also *noblesse oblige*—which in the twentieth century United States is an attempt to lay claim to social superiority by imitating the real or imagined behavior of European aristocrats of past centuries. I am here suggesting that we may also act altruistically when an instinct to help kith and kin is, temporarily or permanently, too difficult or painful to express. And thus may be wonderfully expressed to a stranger. And that which cannot be felt from kith and kin may be received and felt from a stranger.

Warmth's truth

Written for 25 December 2012

Christmas, we might in 2012 say, is also a holy day and also a day of rest. Falling this year on a Tuesday, my blogging day, it has also been for me a day of posting, on Montaigbakhtinian.com. Those who, rather than reading, would be stretched out on a couch or singing songs, opening presents, enjoying a dinner, . . . Well, you will have done those things. Meanwhile, I would touch on two subjects which perhaps a future year will provide opportunities to explore further.

One of these is the troubled subject of love. I was impressed that President Obama, in speaking to the nation after the Newtown shooting, came to these words:

> There's only one thing we can be sure of, and that is the love that we have for our children, for our families, for each other. The warmth of a small child's embrace, that is true.

As a species of philosopher I was impressed to hear a President speaking so philosophically. Of course Presidents and their speechwriters routinely look for first principles (however imaginary or deceptive) on which to ground their proposed actions. Since our forefathers fought for liberty, we should send armies into this or that country to do more fighting for liberty. Or, to quote yet again from one of my favorite speeches, Lyndon Johnson's "Great Society" speech: "The purpose of protecting the life of our Nation and preserving the liberty of our citizens is to pursue the happiness of our people." And, therefore, in the speech's great, now heartbreaking lines, Johnson proposes that the Great Society is a place "where the city of man serves not only the needs of the body and the demands of commerce but the desire for beauty and the hunger for community.

. . . It is a place where men are more concerned with the quality of their goals than the quantity of their goods."

As regards philosophy, Obama and his speechwriters went a step further, not only philosophizing as a means to an end. For a space of about forty words amid two thousand, philosophy itself was the end. Obama was trying to help us, and perhaps himself as well, to find something certain, something true and beautiful, in a world that can seem—that largely is—beyond our control and at times of such harsh beauty. Descartes proposed "cogito, ergo sum" and Obama "The warmth of a small child's embrace, that is true." To paraphrase Keats, that may be all we know on Earth and all we need to know.

I am fortunate to have generous philosopher friends who also responded to Obama's Newtown words and sent me some snippets from other philosophers. From Merleau-Ponty's essay *Lecture de Montaigne*, a line about "regaining the grace of our first certainties in the doubt that rings them round." From Gabriel Marcel (who criticized Descartes's cogito as too self-centered):

> [L]ove treated as the subordination of the self to
> a superior reality, a reality at my deepest level more
> truly me than I am myself—love as the breaking of the
> tension between self and other, appears to me to be
> what one might call the essential ontological datum.

Marcel's words provide a segue to my second subject, which is the "other," though I will often refer to it, oddly enough, under the heading "animal rights." This December I heard on the radio that the state of New Jersey was planning to shoot contraceptives into deer, ostensibly as a way of reducing the deer population in the state without killing any deer in the process. I soon discovered that this was an old story and one that has been much discussed on the Web by hunters, suburbanites and animal rights advocates. Authorities on Fire Island in Long Island Sound have been treating deer in this way for some years already and believe the program has been successful.

Stumbling upon the story this month I was reminded of

two things I had read, one a long time ago and one quite recently. Long ago I read in Tzvetan Todorov's *La Conquête de l'Amérique* a story about residents of a Caribbean island in the sixteenth century, people who believed that after their deaths they would travel to a paradise where not only would life be easy but they would live again with all those who had died before them. The Spanish conquerors wanted these people to peaceably leave their homes and come labor in mines or on sugar plantations on the islands of the Greater Antilles. So they told the people that the Spanish ships were going to take them to the promised land. When, arriving, the people realized that this new place was in fact a kind of hell, and their deceased relatives were not there, the dissonance was so great, many of the people committed suicide, either directly or more slowly, having lost the desire to feed themselves. They could not go on living in a world that was so different from their expectations.

Why did that particular story come to my mind when I heard of New Jersey's plan to shoot contraceptives into deer? I found myself thinking of the does who—at least as I, personifying, imagined it—were going to continue having sex, being penetrated, but who were not going to become pregnant, were not going to produce any offspring. Some of these deer might find themselves parts of herds in which there were no more offspring. It could seem as if the species had come to an end. The world seems to be going on, but not us.

The bit I read quite recently is from David Riesman's *The Lonely Crowd* (originally published in 1950):

> Without the prevention of childbirth by means of postponement of marriage or other contraceptive measures, the [human] population must be limited by taking the life of living beings. And so societies have *invented* cannibalism, induced abortion, organized wars, made human sacrifice, and practiced infanticide (especially female) as means of avoiding periodic famine and epidemics. [Riesman's emphasis.]

Some pages later he adds:

> A whole way of life . . . is the basis of distinction be-
> tween the societies in which human fertility is allowed
> to take its course and toll and those which prefer to pay
> other kinds of toll to cut down on fertility by calcula-
> tion, and, conceivably, as Freud and other observers
> have suggested, by a decline in sexual energy itself.

There are some contradictions and other confusions in these sentences, but the point as regards New Jersey deer is clear. Their lone predator, at least in the suburban counties, is human beings, and so their alternatives are: to become so populous as to be vulnerable to famine and epidemics; to have their populations controlled by human hunters (or a venison industry?); or to cut back on procreative sex, possibly with the help of humans' contraceptive darts. From this perspective the darts may be the best option, and indeed many humans have come to believe in using contraception themselves (or having females use it). It is presumably from this perspective that New Jersey state officials have decided to see how the darts work.

I have been surprised to find myself in middle-age as committed as I am to "animal rights." Doubling back, and perhaps seeming to contradict myself, I will begin this segment by writing of my resistance to aspects of the animal rights agenda. I am not a vegetarian and do not expect to become one. Among other things, my sensibility is such that I do not feel that killing a stalk of wheat is somehow less bad for the wheat than killing a cow is for the cow. An argument against my position could be that cows, or crustaceans, feel pain not unlike we do, and that stalks of wheat do not. And I would say then that it is *also* worth appreciating the validity of the "feelings" or experiences of species and things that do not seem so like us, of species and things that may "feel" in ways we cannot imagine or that may be beyond feeling, without this implying any inferiority.

One may read in the animal ethics literature about "anthropodenial," the refusal to acknowledge that animals share many important mental capacities with humans. And, inversely, one may read about how we have obligations towards animals on account of a "felt kinship." But my interest is not only in similarities, but also in differences. It is a great challenge to recognize that others (to include people with different skin colors or sex organs) are like us. It is a yet larger challenge to acknowledge the otherness of others (be they women, men, deer or rocks) and to respect them for their differences.

More generally, my resistance includes this question: Why is animal rights so important, and in the midst of starving children, abused children, prison rape, capital punishment, the power of capital to channel our responses so that they serve capital rather than human needs? My list could be much longer, and I imagine that readers could add many other items as well. Preventing shooting sprees, in schools in particular, is high on many Americans' lists.

And yet, resistances notwithstanding, something like or well beyond the animal rights agenda has come to seem central to me. That is, I have come to believe strongly that the members of all other species are "ends in themselves." (This is from Kant, *Fundamental Principles of the Metaphysic of Morals*. Here from a translation by T.K. Abbott: "Man and generally any rational being exists as an end in himself, not merely as a means to be arbitrarily used by this or that will".) At the risk of being laughed at, and not afraid of being laughed at, I will add that I even believe there is a way of thinking not only about seemingly a-rational beings, but also about inorganic matter—a way of thinking about rocks and water, for example—as ends in themselves.

I return to my earlier point: It is *also* worth appreciating the validity of the "feelings" or experiences of species and things that do not seem so like us. The New England preacher and theologian Jonathan Edwards once asked his listeners to think of what "the sleeping rocks dream of." He proposed that this will help us "get a complete idea of nothing," and he also gave a sermon titled "Stupid as Stones." I would propose, rather, that thinking of rocks' dreams or possible stupidity is a worthy thought experiment. The Polish poet Zbigniew Herbert wrote (in "Kamyk": The Stone) that stones have "a scent that does not remind one of anything" and:

Kamyki nie dają się oswoić
do końca będą na nas patrzeć
okiem spokojnym bardzo jasnym

Stones cannot be domesticated
to the end they will be looking at us
with calm, very clear eyes

He might well have been thinking of deer, the way they look at us.

All this speaks to one of my interests in the other and in what I am rather approximately referring to as animal rights. Preachers, poets and essay writers notwithstanding, other beings do not exist to help us learn things or to think and feel more deeply, and yet their otherness is, as it were, on offer, and could help lead us to deeper understandings of ourselves as other. As a subscriber to the scientific journal *Nature*, I am weekly confronted by the sadistic practices of medical researchers (growing tumors in mice and so forth). I am aware that sadism has its pleasures; it is, *inter alia*, a way for dependent creatures (e.g. members of a highly social species) to revel in fantasies of autonomy, of not being in any way limited by the feelings or existence of anyone or anything else. But this can have little to do with knowledge, let alone wisdom.

I am blessed on this 25 December 2012 to be able to spend yet another day with Jonah. He is no longer a small child, and in the 12 years we have spent together, he has, among so many other things, helped me appreciate that if there is a future for our science and for our species, it has little to do with laboratory tests on other animals, or with shooting contraceptives into deer. At least in this respect Obama and his speechwriters were pointing the country in a more promising direction. "The warmth of a small child's embrace, that is true."

The speech's preceding sentence about the "one thing we can be sure of" spoke of our adult love for our children and others, but I am more taken by this second claim, by which it is *not* that we adults might, using our rational capacities, come to love our children better, or to better protect them from the wild world in

36

which we play our wild parts. Rather, the proposition is that small children—prior to "*l'âge de raison*" (the age of reason, traditionally age 7)—have this to offer us: warmth's truth.

9

It was a warm, sunny day

A story from a golden age, 2002, before "cellular telephones" (since become cellphones) became more ubiquitous than eyeglasses, and phone booths an endangered species.

It was a warm, sunny day, so during my lunch break I went to the public garden attached to the United Nations. I found an empty bench and began to revise one of my essays. As I was working two American tourists, a young couple, came and sat down on the bench. The woman pulled out her cellular telephone, called some firm and began discussing a delivery she wanted. Her talking made it hard for me to concentrate, but I did not feel I could protest. It wasn't my bench. The woman was just having a conversation (though for some reason one person talking on a telephone is more distracting than two people engaged in conversation face to face. It seems the conversation, the speaker, is in search of an audience; you are being called upon to fill a void.) I was annoyed that this woman seemed completely unconcerned that she might be disturbing me.

She got off the phone, and the young man took a few snapshots. In the accepted-as-polite manner he asked if I would be willing to take a picture of the two of them.

"No!" I said, departing radically from the customary, "polite" script.

"No?" He was astonished.

"Well, you all sat down here and started talking on the phone, which disturbed my writing. So I hardly feel inclined to take a picture of you."

He was astounded. "This is a public park," he said.

"Yes," I said. "And I am a member of the public."

"If you want to write, you should go to an office," he said.

"And if you want to talk on the telephone, you should use a phone booth."

He couldn't believe I could be so obtuse. He called me a "fucking asshole" and told me to get my head out of my ass. I replied in kind. Finally he walked off, with a last retort—"old fart."

This I registered as a rite of passage. It was the first time in my life I had been called an "old fart," and I looked in the mirror afterward to see how old I appeared. However, I thought more about the obtuseness of this young couple, and about how common such obtuseness is in New York, and perhaps throughout the United States and in other parts of the world. (These two tourists, after all, were not from New York.)

When these people sat down on the bench they noticed me but gave not a thought to how they might be affecting me, what my needs might be. Until they saw that I could be of use. Whereupon they approached me politely, and from their perspective this fact— their politeness—entitled them to service and made me a bad person for not providing it.

This may seem—is—a stretch, however, this incident became linked in my mind with a *New York Times* article about relations between the United States and the people of the Marshall Islands. Apparently, toward the end of the twentieth century Americans were feeling baffled and offended by the Marshall Islanders' resentment of them. We had given them some $1 billion in aid— what could be more polite, more generous than that? "Something went badly wrong," the reporter wrote, "for usually it is possible to be resented without paying $1 billion for the privilege."

What the reporter glossed over was the source of this resentment: how, in the course of our development of our nuclear arsenal, we dropped numerous nuclear bombs on these islands, obliterating some of them. One day in 1954 we dropped a bomb—"Bravo"!—that exceeded the combined strength of all the weapons fired in the history of humankind. And as part of all this we exposed local residents to toxic levels of radiation. (Thus our generosity: Marshall Islanders who have come down with leukemia have been given $125,000.)

Nor was the radiation poisoning a tragic mistake. Before the bomb tests were conducted scientists had realized that atomic radiation, including from nuclear-weapons tests, would have dire health consequences. This is why the bombs were dropped on these distant, foreign islands rather than in a remote part of the United States. And the bombs once dropped, the Marshall Islanders, without their knowledge, became test subjects for studies of the effects of atomic radiation on human beings. A comment Marshall Islanders have been having trouble forgetting, made by an Atomic Energy Commission manager to a U.S. Congressional hearing in 1956: "Data of this type has never been available. While it is true that these people do not live, I would say, the way Westerners do, civilized people, it is nevertheless true that these people are more like us than the mice."

I am tempted to write self-righteously about how, as some uses of other human beings are less noxious than others, so are some uses of public space. A writer or reader is quiet; users of electronic devices make noise. However, I have noticed that most Americans are less disturbed by cellphones and even boomboxes than by the sight of someone writing or reading in a park, restaurant or other place to which they have come to relax. The Russian-French philosopher Vladimir Jankélévitch has written about how human beings have long tried to make sounds (music, conversation) to escape from their anxieties and the seeming silence of the universe and of eternity. Jankélévitch draws an analogy with a traveler lost at night who speaks out loud and laughs loudly in order to persuade himself that he is not afraid. Thanks to the protective screen of the sounds he is making, the traveler imagines that he is even scaring away the specter of death. ("I sing, as the Boy does by the Burying Ground — because I am afraid": Emily Dickinson.)

These notes suggest why it makes Americans uneasy to see someone working quietly by himself or herself. We might imagine that it is yet worse if this someone is working on a narrative, a history, or on an analysis of past experiences. We came to this continent to escape the shackles of the past, and we now fear and resent attempts to re-shackle us, as it were, to our own past, to what we have done as Americans, to include dropping bombs on other people.

10

Zeroing in

Variations on a possible aphorism

This will be an unusual, oddly (usefully?) repetitive, experimental piece. I had an idea. At first it seemed an idea for one of my aphorisms. Then, late one night, as I was hoping to get past thoughts and hopes to sleep, the idea began to expand and speak of something more general, something about being a human being and interacting with other human beings, at least in the corner of the twenty-first century "Western" world in which I find myself.

I trust that in time I will understand better what this idea is telling me and how the details work themselves out in daily life (including in work and family relationships and romantic ones). Among other things, the "I" needs to be better integrated; the "I" cannot be much different from the many other human beings he is (I am) describing. And—avoiding making a complex set of "variations" yet more complex—I am ignoring what the Shakespeare scholar Harold Bloom has named "self-overhearing," the fact that sometimes when we speak or reflect, a part of our self overhears what we are saying and may form independent judgments of what we are saying and why. And insofar as the focus of the present text is on the parallel universes of the under-sensitive (or the ignoring, the denying) and the over-sensitive, it should be noted that forests and even trees may be missed by those with an eye for individual fungi, Lady Slippers, spider webs.

The Variations

1 How could I have known this is what you wanted—because you never mentioned it?

2 The role of imagination in sensation may be underestimated.

The highly sensitive may add imagination to sensation and thus perceive things, present and not present, that others cannot.

3   People express their desires reasonably clearly, but often they will not hear what their words are saying. If you respond to what has been expressed, it may seem to be you who is confused.

> 3a   People express their desires reasonably clearly, but often they will not hear what their words and deeds are saying. If you respond to what has been expressed, you may end up the more confused.

4   If you respond directly to desires, positive and negative, that other people's words and deeds express, they may well deny having ever felt or expressed what you have so clearly heard.

5   Suppose you continued to listen carefully to what people were saying, and in particular to the desires they expressed, but you responded as if they had said the opposite. Would you live in greater harmony?

6   A way to live quite confused is to listen carefully to what other people are saying and to respond as if they, too, were listening to themselves.

> 6a   A way to live quite confused is to listen carefully to what other people are saying and watch what they are doing, and to respond as if they, too, noticed or cared to.

7   A careful listener surrounded by people who cannot hear what they are saying or why they are saying such things will receive many signals to which he cannot respond.

> 7a   To live in a Freudian world surrounded by non-Freudians involves receiving many messages and not being able to respond to any.
> 7b   A Freudian surrounded by non-Freudians receives many

messages that people will deny ever sending.

8   Many people go through life lying, to themselves above all, about who they are, what they are doing and what they want. If you, taken in or not, respond to this stuff as if it had some positive connection to truth, any temporary confusion will be lessened and these other people will understand and appreciate you.

9   People speak quite clearly and in many different ways, but if you respond directly to what they are saying you will be alone.

10   Is it possible that any given person, to include the author of these lines, could be more honest either about himself or with other people? And if so, in what confusion would he live?

III

The Practice of Philosophy

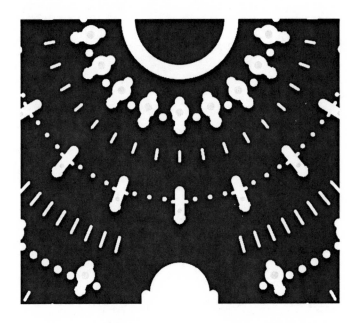

[T]o be is to be for the other and with the other. Put otherwise, to be is to be in dialogue.

—Dmitri Nikulin, *On Dialogue*

On just being

Clarifying, I note that the title uses the word "just" in the sense of "merely," "only"—"just another manic Monday"—and not in the sense of "justice." At the same time I note that this essay risks descending into sophistry, and this may be exemplified by the possibility of now proposing that just being could be the most just way to be.

When I was thinking about this piece I had lunch with a French actress for whom my "just being" recalled the idea that we should live in the moment. This led me to dig up the long famous line from Horace: "dum loquimur, fugerit invida aetas: carpe diem, quam minimum credula postero." While we are speaking (and eating and digging up old Odes), envious time will have fled. And so—and instead, in some way?—we should seize the day, trusting as little as possible in the future. Which means? My friend and I should have gone back to her apartment, slipped off our clothes, spent the rest of the afternoon, or of our lives, in bed?

One of the glitches here is connected to this word "should," which is intimately connected to the *ur* question of how to live: What should I do? What should I do—write—right now? My sense is that my friend and I were closer to just being when we were rather aimlessly eating crepes, drinking wine and talking about my essay and her interest in Judaism than we would have been if we had started trying to seize the day or thinking about shoulds.

That said, I also note that this question of what should I do/how should "I" live underlies all human conversation. "Where should we go for dinner?" "How're you making out on your homework?" "Did the Yankees win?" "Do you think this shirt looks good on me?" Paraphrasing a line from Sartre's *L'être et le néant* (Being and Nothingness), we might say that our conversations make shoulds, assertions of the right way to live (enjoying a good meal, doing our homework, winning, looking good)—spring up like partridges.

I also have the sense that these days, in response to our lives of these past several hundred years and to the many pressing, but seemingly trivial demands of twenty-first century life, there is an idea that "just being" or something like it might be *the* or an answer. How should "I" live (presuming my food and shelter are provided for)? Just be.

D avid Levy, a former Palo Alto computer scientist who now teaches a course on "information and the quality of life," has written about how in the 1920s the US business community became concerned by modern technology's ability to produce more than consumers needed or even felt they needed. Labor leaders proposed reducing the work week, and this period saw such wonderful innovations as the weekend. But then business leaders, with help from the growing advertising industry, discovered, as one report put it, "that one want satisfied makes way for another . . . [W]e have a boundless field before us; . . . there are new wants which will make way endlessly for newer wants". Goodie goodie for Steve Jobs and Palo Alto, but not for just being?

In the same article ("No Time to Think") Levy also quotes from the Nobel-Prize-winning cytogeneticist Barbara McClintock's oft-quoted description of getting so into her studies of the insides of corn cells, she forgot herself and where she was. "[T]he more I worked with [the chromosomes] the bigger and bigger they got, and when I was really working with them, I wasn't outside, I was down there, I was part of the system. . . . These were my friends."

Of course we cannot call this just being, because, in our acquisitive age, McClintock was trying to get something from the chromosomes: knowledge. And there is her line about friendship which could send us back to the Old Testament and its equating of knowledge and penetration (sex). All this is more, and thus also less, than just being.

Nonetheless, the McClintock example may suggest what our goal is: to be fully on the inside of our lives. With this, un-McClintockian and un-Levyian amendment: Just being would involve being on the inside without realizing that this was where we were. Making love without realizing we were making anything at all.

A long, long time ago—"I can still remember how that music used to make me smile". Or, another pop line, "Prepare yourself, you know it's a must, Gotta have a friend in Jesus." The restaurants in which I do my writing are often playing old pop songs to enhance my dining or writing experience. And while neither waxing nostalgic nor turning to an other—for example, to Jesus, for help getting into heaven—seem to have much to do with just being, this morning the songs have brought on nostalgia.

A long, long time ago my first wife and I sold our lease on a New York loft and went to Paris to enjoy a year of writing, making art, learning French, being in Paris. This was back before the Internet, etc.; the whole year we made one phone call back to the States, that one at Christmas from a booth at the central post office. Instead we wrote letters, and I suppose our letters were full of news of all the things we were doing, and this led my mother, in one of her return letters, to write something like, "Don't forget to save some time to just be." And thus, we might say, an essay—this essay—was conceived, though the gestation took 30 years.

The idea has stuck in my mind not least because I consider myself someone who spends extremely little time just being. For instance, every year Jonah and I take a February vacation, and I bring along a collection of books and greatly look forward to lingering over breakfast reading and reading, and then reading again over lunch and dinner. (Jonah is a bigger reader than I am.) It has not been lost on me that this reading is, from one perspective, a way of not being fully on vacation, of not simply being in the balmy air, next to the sea, next to Jonah. Would we say then that the people who by 9 a.m. are completely creamed and horizontal in a poolside *chaise longue*—they know, or at least know better than Jonah and I do, how to just be?

These people's idea of just being (or of just being on vacation) seems not all that far from my mother's. That is, in our not only acquisitive but also productivity obsessed age, just being is defined

49

negatively: not working, not learning, not thinking even, and perhaps not even feeling. In my mother's case, I think that her idea was that my wife Molly and I might spend less time producing and learning things and more time enjoying the beauty of Paris and its great food and museums. As a downwardly mobile person, I am tempted to call this the downwardly mobile version of just being— what one can do with a little money and if you have little interest in duplicating the amassing and social climbing of your ancestors.

Paris brings Baudelaire's *flâneur* (saunterer or loafer) to mind.

> La foule est son domaine, comme l'air est celui de l'oiseau, . . .

> The crowd is his element, as the air for birds and water for fish. His passion and his profession are to marry himself with the crowd. For the perfect *flâneur*, for the passionate spectator, there is an ecstasy in being part of the multitude, a part of the ebb and flow, of the fleeting and infinite. To be away from home and yet to feel oneself everywhere at home; to see the world, to be at the center of the world, and yet to remain hidden from the world . . .

The text quoted here (« Le peintre de la vie moderne », 1863) is not, however, about how to "just be"; it champions a different response to modern life. Baudelaire goes on to say that his ideal man has a higher and wider goal than just being *un flâneur*. Beyond the fleeting pleasures of the moment, such a man wants to find the poetry in the modern moment and its fashions, to extract the eternal from the transitory. Like Baudelaire we remain prey to the values of the Enlightenment and of the Industrial Revolution, in which in the end something must be learned or produced, and even delicious idleness must be justified by some tangible, socially useful or otherwise exaltable outcome.

And is not using electronic devices to track down vaguely remembered texts, and this to write an essay about "just being"—is this not one of the myriad ways we just are? Our poetry is, after all, just poetry; our vacations just vacations; our moments of ecstasy just moments of ecstasy. (And, sadly, how quickly they are forgotten, or how sad that what we remember is the fact, and not the feelings.) To twist another phrase of Sartre's, human beings would seem to be, and like all other entities, condemned to just be. If just be-ers can be said to be capable of making mistakes, our error would *not* be in failing so often to just be, but rather in failing to see that what we are always doing is just being? Or is failing to see the key to just being?

I have an ongoing interest in human ignorance, both in the prevalence and inescapability of it, and also in our attachment to ignorance. Thus I note that lying in the sun poolside at 9 a.m. on a Tuesday morning is less just being if it includes being aware that one is lying in the sun poolside at 9 a.m. on a Tuesday morning. (To say nothing of *working* on one's tan. And nowadays such poolside liers are also often on their smartphones texting their friends: "Guess where I am? Jamaica!")

I am tempted to rename this essay "On just quoting." In my New York restaurant, which, as I have been writing, has itself been steadily filling up with just brunchers whose chatter has buried the Golden Oldies, I have searched in my computer files for two quotations from the German sociologist Georg Simmel:

> [P]eople talk seriously because of some content they want to communicate or come to an understanding about, while at a social gathering they talk for the sake of talking. . . .

> The essence of the blasé attitude consists in the bluntness of discrimination. This does not mean that the objects are not perceived, as is the case with the half-wit, but rather that the meaning and differing values of things, and thereby the things themselves, are experienced as insubstantial. They appear to the blasé person in an evenly flat and gray tone; no one object deserves preference over any other.

The second quotation sounds like a description of depression, while its "bluntness of discrimination" approaches my ideas of just being as all-encompassing and as involving not noticing. And my sense is that the first quotation, too, touches on just being, on one particular form of it. But I have now made an assumption that I suspect is false: that something like just being could have different forms or any form at all. Were that assumption true, I might go on to say that this morning—that is, in an hour before I began drafting this essay—I was just lying in bed, not so much to get more rest or to prepare to write, reflect on my life or listen to the first birds of spring; I was just lying in bed. And, now—at this moment and in my life in general, now that I have gone beyond the career-enthralled years of a modern human life—when I write I may be more just writing than trying to produce anything (let alone trying to preach anything—how to live?).

I cannot say, however, that I have entirely renounced Baudelaire's *tirer l'éternel*—trying to extract the eternal from the flux—but often these days writing seems to be, above all, a drug. Perhaps the endorphins, or whatever they are, come from a McClintock-like insidedness, though with an added dose of *nombrilisme*—of self-absorption or narcissism. Or let's call it a befriending of myself. But this is to write again of products, results, feelings. The goal of this essay was to explore just being and this, ideally, would itself be a way of just being.

12

The practice of philosophy

A friend told me that every morning upon waking she meditates for an hour. My first reaction to this news was not positive. First thing in the morning nothing has yet happened, I thought to myself, and yet already this person, my friend, wants to distance herself from the nothingness or prepare herself to remain at arm's length from the anything or nothing that might happen later in the day.

I take my reaction to be both to lengthy morning meditation and to the many morning hours I myself have spent on this essay and on many another text. For me, meditating upon waking, which I have tried, is annoying. First thing in the morning there is nothing I want more than to get out of my apartment, breathe the fresher air outside in the park-like area in which I live. I want to get to a restaurant to get my coffee and get down to work: to reading and writing (for example, about the possibility of meditating instead).

Astrid, let's call her—my friend—is not only a devoted practitioner of meditation and yoga and related disciplines, she proselytizes for them. She thinks that my life would be better—happier and more elevated, perhaps not so ready to remind her of pleasures of the flesh—were I to take up meditation. (*N.B.:* This would be re-taking-up the Transcendental Meditation I tried during college and occasionally after that, or expanding on the few minutes of meditating I do in between my treadmill runs, stretches and naps.) For Astrid, meditation and yoga have served as a solution—provisional most likely—to the problems of life and of her life in particular.

But, I asked have myself, what kind of solution is this if it takes up all of your time? An hour each morning, then doing and teaching yoga in the afternoons and evenings, and weekend workshops and so forth. The solution to the problem of mortality turns out to be spending all the time one is allotted trying to solve the problem of mortality? To quote, quite out of context, two lines from a poem read recently:

> I am wondering how we live at all
> Or if we do.

It is often the case with me that an initial negative reaction is a sign that there is something I might learn from reconsidering, in a more positive light, the rejected words or experience. And this little comment by my friend about her meditating has proved an excellent example of how resistance (be it mine or another's) can often be a bass-akward call to not push away but explore. (I can't help feeling that *philia* and *eros*—attraction, love, sex—linger in the shadows of this piece, as does *thanatos*, death. Therein lie the anxiety-provoking nothings and somethings that drive us to meditate, write, get drunk, so many things.)

I have been working on another essay about both *philia* and writing, an essay exploring Plato's *Lysis*, but also bringing me back to the *Phaedo*, Plato's version of Socrates's last hours, before he drank the hemlock. This work mixing with my friend's news led me to realize that long ago Socrates had hit upon a solution not unlike that of my friend's. Socrates's solution was more social, more verbal—talking to other people, getting caught up in words and what they might mean, rather than focusing inwardly on muscles and organs, and on breathing, trying to let go of words, thoughts, meanings. But Plato's Socrates's practice also needed or merited frequent repeating and took up the best hours of his days. And it might be said to have taken his life.

Prior to this little light bulb going on in my head I had for years been thinking and writing about Americans' and other human beings' relentless quest for a solution to the human predicament—our mortality, our interdependence, the weight of consciousness, the confusions of language, our desperation to create and preserve an illusory sense of order to avoid the ambient madness. Astrid's meditating helped me see that my idea of a solution had been too narrow. I had been thinking of it as an answer to a question, a putative right answer. This narrowness was hardly unique to me. We have come back again to one of the fundamental questions of philosophy, of ethics: How to live? What should "I" do in some larger sense or right now? Which keyboard key to tap, when to stop writing and go to the Y, get on the treadmill? Thousands upon thousands of pages have been written proposing and criticizing answers to these questions. And this is also what Astrid was urging upon me, a particular answer. How to live? Meditate an hour every morning. Yoga in the afternoons and evenings.

But, you might say, what I was finally able to hear in all this was not the "meditate" part, but the "every morning." The answer—or the non-answer, if you prefer—is a practice. You might "get it," realize the true path, but this is only the beginning. Now, in order for the solution to work, you have to walk this path daily.

A contrast may illustrate my point here. In Paul's road-to-Damascus vision of Christianity and of salvation (of "the solution"), one suddenly sees the Light, realizes the truth, and thus one is saved. The struggle is over (backsliding excepted). But for Plato's Socrates the Light may indeed be shining in another realm, but it cannot be seen by us. What the example of Socrates's practice shows, however, is that engaging in conversation related to this Light, to our desire to see it, to our faint ideas about its nature and the shadows that it casts, and—here is what I want to italicize—*by engaging repeatedly in this conversation*, human beings, or some human beings, can find relief. (*Cf.* Sextus Empiricus's description of skepticism as involving doggedly setting out "oppositions among things," and thereby coming "first to suspension of judgment and afterwards to tranquility.")

In Plato's dialogues it is often *philia*, most specifically physical attraction to beautiful young men, that inspires Socrates to enter into conversations, and with these young men first and foremost. Another might find his or her relief in trying to have sex with other people. But Socrates's practice—which has been called Socratic intellectualism, and which I am also here calling the *practice* of philosophy—involves a turning away from the physical, a repressing or sublimating of instincts and feelings. There is a sense in which Socrates is trying to seduce others, to draw them into his light or shadows, into one of his repetitive conversations. But at another level it is not feelings of love or power that he is after. Instead he wants to talk about what love or power might be and what knowledge (e.g. of love or power) might be. Instead of the pleasures of physical rubbing of one kind or another, he engages in verbal rubbing, in *elenchus* (refutation via cross-examination) and dialectic.

From this perspective I take my own practice and Plato's and other writers' as being more disembodied, distant and bloodless. "O fearful meditation!" Shakespeare, in sonnet 65, writes, while reflecting on "sad mortality" and Time's "wreckful siege." He notes that the writer's solution—the writer's escape from such meditations, if not from meditation more generally—involves placing faith in the possibility "that in black ink my love may still shine bright." This is not the same as loving, or as engaging in love, nor is it the same as talking with others about love. We writers are, at least while writing—while making sand castles of words?—largely lost to either social or physical practices. And, returning to Astrid's meditation, we might now say that hers is a more physical practice than either writing or talking, but it shares writing's isolation and self-centeredness, and also takes Socratic repression or sublimation a few steps further—to letting go. I am sure Astrid would not say this, but we might wonder if love, power and knowledge are among the things being let go of during meditation. Or being said good-bye to?

Sensing the end of this particular journey, I would call attention to some tensions that exist currently in the practice of philosophy—in the study, teaching and writing of it, particularly by professors and their students. A century ago, Anglo-Saxon philosophy began to be quite taken or overwhelmed by the stunning discoveries of modern science. Dominant voices in Anglo-Saxon philosophy have expressed both a sense of belittlement, as if philosophy could now only be a handmaiden to science, and also an enthusiasm for reforming philosophy's ways, adopting modern scientific practices, to include building philosophical knowledge through linguistic or logical investigations, discovery building on discovery. It may well be that we, our scientists included, will never achieve The Truth (or what the present essay has been calling "the solution"), but if we keep working diligently and sensibly, we will keep climbing the mountain. This is the belief in any case.

Which ignores, for instance, Montaigne's insight: « Nous ne sommes non plus près du ciel sur le Mont-Cenis qu'au fond de la mer. » Nor are we closer to heaven on the top of Mount Cenis than at the bottom of the sea. Ignored, too, is the rather large obstacle that the philosopher of physics Michael Redhead, among others, has called attention to: "To understand anything requires us to understand everything." Seemingly fundamental concepts— gravity, e=mc² —as simple, elegant and useful in making technical predictions as they are—are also meaningless until we know how they fit into some all-comprehending whole, assuming such a concept itself has any meaning.

The universe is written in the language of mathematics; "l'universo e' scritto in linguaggio matematico," Galileo famously wrote. It may not be all that long before we come to see this as "but the objectification of the mood of an age, perhaps fitful and temporary, rather than the reasoned expression of the intellectual insight of all ages" (E.A. Burtt, *The Metaphysical Foundations of Modern Science*). Mathematics, like its cousin music, certainly inspires hearts and minds, but in some future it may seem to not well describe either the realms in which we live or the universe of which these realms would seem to form but a part. Certainly the visions of many religions—e.g. of Buddhist texts—can cast our math and science in this light. A day may come when we realize (rightly or wrongly) that our mountains of modern knowledge, or information, are, like these words, a kind of sand. And this will not eliminate the fact that we and our ancestors have been doing a lot of climbing, have exhausted ourselves with all our climbing in such sands, hoping against hope that some Mount Cenis will indeed prove closer to heaven than to the bottom of the sea. In the future it may become clearer that this climbing is one of our practices, one of the most time-consuming "solutions" we have yet found: climbing in and with the sands of knowledge and information— investigating, making discoveries, devising formulas, competing for Nobel Prizes, . . .

Another tension is between, on the one hand, the road-to-Damascus idea of a solution or discovery (e.g. a cure for cancer or for mortality) that in a flash resolves all problems (death loses its "sting") and, on the other hand, the idea of a regular practice that brings some relief. As regards the first of these possibilities, see Augustine's wish to find "pacem sine vespera" (the peace that has no evening), and these lines from Wittgenstein's Augustine-inspired *Philosophical Investigations*, §133:

> The real discovery is the one that makes me capable
> of stopping doing philosophy when I want to.—The
> one that gives philosophy peace, so that it is no longer
> tormented by questions which bring itself in question.

The structure, the compulsiveness, the restless internal dialogue of the *Investigations* proposes, however, that any such "real discovery" is an illusion. It is what Kant called a *focus imaginarius*— "not only for clarifying the confused play of things human, . . . but for giving a consoling view of the future". In pursuing the illusion we engage—in black ink or pixels, in study and conversation, in science, philosophy and religion—in practices that do give us some peace, temporarily.

In the world of academic philosophy, people take classes and go to talks and conferences, they write and read, exploring many "solutions," many answers. Thereby, *inter alia*, they help keep us from forgetting that the basic questions remain—thank God!— unanswerable. (Were a most brilliant philosopher, scientist, mystic, or some series of them to indeed come up with the solution, they'd wreck the whole game. Which is also to say that they would show themselves quite lacking in brilliance, quite unable to appreciate what philosophy, science and religion are most fundamentally concerned with, the purposes they serve and how.)

No "real solution" can be found. Others (and philosophers too) take drugs, have sex, play cards, make art. What is found, again and again, is relief, temporary relief. The sleep after making love with another human being and before one feels the desire, then the strong desire, then the need to rejoin in love—or to again gamble, take a pill, sculpt, turn on the computer, find someone to talk philosophy with.

One of the analogies that has informed this piece is of children at the seashore building and rebuilding forts, channels and dams. The waves keep coming to overwhelm and wash away their constructions. And they yell joyfully, "Work harder!" "We've got to keep digging!" And the afternoon passes warm and wet.

Notes for avid readers

1   "I am wondering . . . " is from the Canadian poet Erin Mouré's "Thirteen Years," as reproduced in J. Paul Hunter, *The Norton Introduction to* Poetry, Sixth Edition (W.W. Norton, 1973).

2   Galileo's proposal, "l'universo e' scritto in linguaggio matematico," appears in *Il Saggiatore* (The Assayer). From Stillman Drake's translation in Galileo, et al., *The Controversy on the Comets of 1618* (University of Pennsylvania Press, 1960):

> Philosophy is written in a grand book—I mean the universe—which stands continuously open to our gaze, but it cannot be understood unless one first learns to comprehend the language and interpret the characters in which it is written. It is written in the language of mathematics, and its characters are triangles, circles, and other geometrical figures, without which it is humanly impossible to understand a single word of it; without these one is wandering about in a dark labyrinth.

3   *Cf.* the French writer Isabelle Sorente's *Addiction générale*, the following being a translation of cover copy for the book:

> We are in the grip of calculations. From the square footage of our homes, through our iron levels, the resolution of our TV screens, the memory of our computers, right up to the financial cost of global warming—everything that concerns us gets turned into numbers. We turn the body into a weight, intelligence into a test result, the past into a genetic code and our anxieties into insurance policies and risk assessments. Here is what we mistakenly call realism: this obsessive resorting to numbers, without which our perceptions as well as our thoughts have come to seem invalid.

4   The sentences regarding Kant's *focus imaginarius* are an amalgam. The second part is from Kant's essay *Idee zu einer allgemeinen Geschichte in weltbürgerlicher Absicht* (Idea for a Universal History from a Cosmopolitan Point of View), as translated by Lewis White Beck; see *Kant: On History* (Pearson, 1963). The phrase *focus imaginarius* appears in the following segment on pages A644/B672-A645/B673 of the *Critique of Pure Reason*, here as translated by Norman Kemp Smith (Modern Library, 1958):

> I accordingly maintain that transcendental ideas never allow of any constitutive employment. When regarded in that mistaken manner, and therefore as supplying concepts of certain objects, they are but pseudo-rational, merely dialectical concepts. On the other hand, they have an excellent, and indeed indispensably necessary, regulative employment, namely, that of directing the understanding towards a certain goal upon which routes marked out by all its rules converge, as upon their point of intersection. This point is indeed a mere idea, a *focus imaginarius*, from which, since it lies quite outside the bounds of possible experience, the concepts of the understanding do not in reality proceed; none the less it serves to give these concepts the greatest [possible] unity combined with the greatest [possible] extension. Hence arises the illusion that the lines have their source in a real object lying outside the

field of empirically possible knowledge—just as objects reflected in a mirror are seen as behind it.

5   Coming at this subject from another angle, in an essay "Exploring our hopes for a cure, with help from *The King's Speech (Zeteo,* Fall 2012)," I wrote about a psychotherapist who had a simple realism. My "problems," he explained and helped me appreciate in various ways, stemmed from some combination of the terms of life, the terms of modern life and my personality and tastes. In this context I had made certain choices. Perhaps they were "only choices," which I could make only one way. Given the opportunity, and now with better knowledge of the consequences, probably I would do similar thinking and make the same choices again, and again.

For all I greatly appreciated this therapy, and the kind of confidence it gave me, I did not appreciate that it made further therapeutic conversation seem pointless. I had to find another therapist who was less conclusive. So that the practice—here of reflection with the help of a devoted (paid) listener—did not come to an end.

13

In winter

At times when driving, I have not only felt sleepy but have felt, as the saying goes, "lulled to sleep." In these moments I have not pictured some horrible car crash that might result, nor the deaths or maiming of the other passengers in my car. It has been a sweet, gentle, peaceful feeling, and at least some of this has come from a sense of finality. This is not a nap I am being lulled to take, but the final sleep. (Reports of some people who have almost frozen to death suggest that when the body shuts down there is a sensation of warmth.)

I have never gotten in an accident, and in fact it has been some years since I have done much driving, but now, approaching 60, I find myself taking a lot of short naps, sometimes twice a day. I nap after working out at the Y, and at home on the couch weekend afternoons, and weekdays at my office, too. I have a colleague from the Middle East who has an interior, windowless office which is decorated with pictures of her three daughters and scented with a light, floral scent, as if by smokeless incense or an open vial of oil. She goes home early and has kindly allowed me to come in her office after she leaves. I lie down on her carpet in the dark, with the scent and sense of her female, motherly presence surrounding me, or standing wool-skirted—too far to touch, unable to be seen—legs parted above me. In a series of stages, as if slipping from ledges, shifting from consciousness of this woman, women, office work, any number of other people and details; a way is made to dreams and to vacant time, absent from my self and from memory.

Playing card games with Jonah during the Christmas holidays, I am struck—overwhelmed, cornered you might say—by his aggressiveness, his relentless commitment to coming out on top, beating not only his aging Papa, but his mother and grandmother as well. I do my best to give him some competition, and for some reason at the card game "Spit"—which would seem a young person's game, demanding quick reflexes and visual acuity—I am still able to more than hold my own. But in a larger sense I am beaten. I don't know that I ever had the level of testosterone that Jonah, 12 years old, now seems to have, and if I did, . . . Now I am more drawn to naps. I have always liked napping, but now it is a need, an increasingly "important" part of my life.

Life is a struggle, and we are programed by our hormones and by other aspects of the machinery to struggle, to try to stay warm and well fed and to keep ourselves safe from harm. We struggle too—does this come from sexual difference and reproduction, our desire to distinguish ourselves, to be desirable to others? We struggle for distinction, to be a person who wins at games or writes interesting essays or has a particularly appealing smell. We are, let's say, deathly afraid of weakness and failure.

But, it seems to me as I take and enjoy my little naps, that along with this fear there also comes a desire to give up, to stop struggling; the desire to rejoin the warmer darkness.

14

On just playing

1   Jonah, now 12, has a problem. He loves to compete, he loves to play sports, he loves being part of teams, and his world offers plenty of opportunities to do these things. But these opportunities tend to involve signing up to be on school teams and "travel teams" with complex sets of schedules of games and practices, and all this run by adults who like giving orders and demanding quiet and prompt attendance and so forth. And Jonah's desire, which seems quite natural for a 12-year-old, is to play. Or, as I have termed it, to "just play."

One might write about how Jonah's problem is a result of having "helicopter parents"—often hovering, like Jonah's mother and me. One might write more generally about how this lack of opportunities to just play, out of sight of adults, is a sad aspect of many American children's lives today. I am also interested in how this lack of "just playing" is also a sad aspect of adult lives today. We may play tennis, which offers an ideal form of social interaction, but often we mix our playing with instruction. It is as if, in New York City at least, we do not feel comfortable saying directly, "I am looking for someone to play with." It is easier if we bump into someones in the midst of some kind of lesson, chaperoned by a personable instructor—*un GO, Gentil Organisateur* (Friendly Organizer), as Club Med titled the role. Similarly with exercise and dance classes and yoga (and not dissimilarly with drawing classes, singing groups, . . .). We are brought together under the rubric of self-improvement and with an animator (to borrow another word from French) who mixes encouragement and instruction (and, at times, demands: try harder). I wonder if one might write similarly about the S&M scene. All the paraphernalia, the roles and jargon allow people lacking an ability to just play to instead play act—to act at playing.

Recently returned to New York after a month in Paris, I went to a discussion and tasting of French wines. We sat at desk-like tables, and nothing but wine and water was on offer (though I was eventually able to get hold of some bread). Some of the attendees were taking notes, either for professional purposes or just out of habit, to give themselves something to do in between sips. All of us were paying inordinate attention to the qualities of the liquids we were sampling. And it struck me that in this way we were completely lost to wine, to its traditional role in society and as part of a meal. Wines have long been crafted to heighten our experience of certain foods at certain times and also to promote certain convivial kinds of social interactions (and also as a way of storing agricultural produce out of season and for protection against bad years, bad harvests). Now, in contemporary New York and many other cities, wines are also used, and perhaps some are crafted to be used, in this odd form of social interaction in which strangers, not in the wine business, come together to taste and learn. Of course many people who go to wine-tastings are also, as I was, interested in the social interaction and may be hoping to "meet someone"—someone who shares their tastes. We might compare this behavior with that of people who go to bars to drink and meet other people. There is a sense in which the bar-goers are coming closer to just playing, and a sense in both cases that an activity that requires intoxicants cannot be "just playing."

2   When I was in Paris I had dinner with an American friend who has, as she herself put it, "food issues." She can no longer eat red meat, eggs, foods with gluten in them, dairy products, . . . In her youth she had always been a bit *rondelette* (pleasingly plump, not at all fat). Now she is bone thin with translucent skin, beautiful in a rare-bird sort of way, but there is also a sense in which she is slowly but surely starving herself. I recalled that one of her grandmothers, in old age, no longer wishing to live, stopped eating.

As we enjoyed a delicious dinner of foods that my friend could eat and that she had carefully prepared, she told about when she had started having these food issues. A divorced mother with one child, there had been a moment when she took her son to college, driving across the United States with him. After she had left him in his dorm room and was driving back the other way she suddenly became violently ill. We could say that at this moment a new life began, a life in which many things formerly taken for granted were no longer possible. And this precisely at the moment when it might have seemed that, with the bulk of the tasks of parenting completed, many new things had suddenly become possible, and when activities renounced while her son was at home could now be resumed.

I have been impressed, more generally, by how the current extraordinary appearance of food issues, or allergies, means that people are now rejecting the staples on which hominids, or human beings in the West at least, have depended for thousands if not millions of years: bread, milk, nuts, meat. May I be excused for interrupting this essay with an extensive quotation from a *Nature* article, "Archaeology: The milk revolution" (31 July 2013). The author, Andrew Curry, reports that 8,000 or so years ago,

> a genetic mutation spread through Europe that gave people the ability to produce lactase—and drink milk—throughout their lives. That adaptation opened up a rich new source of nutrition that could have sustained communities when harvests failed. This two-step milk revolution may have been a prime factor in allowing bands of farmers and herders from the south to sweep through Europe and displace the hunter-gatherer cultures that had lived there for millennia.

Curry quotes Mark Thomas, a population geneticist at University College London, proposing that a large proportion of Europeans could be descended from the first dairy farmers in Europe who took advantage of the genetic mutation, which offered a major selective advantage.

> In a 2004 study, researchers estimated that people with the mutation would have produced up to 19% more fertile offspring than those who lacked it. The researchers called that degree of selection "among the strongest yet seen for any gene in the genome". Compounded

over several hundred generations, that advantage could help a population to take over a continent. But only if "the population has a supply of fresh milk and is dairying", says Thomas. . . .

Dairy products—which could be stored for longer in colder climes—provided rich sources of calories that were independent of growing seasons or bad harvests.

Others think that milk may have helped, particularly in the north, because of its relatively high concentration of vitamin D, a nutrient that can help to ward off diseases such as rickets.

One can also be impressed by an immigrant to France who does not eat bread or cheese. Is this like me in New York, not liking either hamburgers or pizza? It is curious, too, that in New York I rarely drink wine with my meals on the grounds that it will interfere with my concentration or with the sleep I need so that I can concentrate. In France I rarely have lunch or dinner without a glass, which is much appreciated and does not seem to have much effect on my powers of concentration or sleep.

How much have I learned from Jonah. How blessed I have been to be able to enjoy his company these many years. Recently he has become re-interested in Yu-Gi-Oh! cards. He had a collection of these "monster," "spell" and "trap" cards years ago and gave them all away as little kids' stuff. But then a friend got him interested in fighting mock battles using these cards—a game in which millions of kids and adults are involved, to include at public gatherings and online. Now Jonah is again collecting the cards and always has a thick pack in his pocket and can spend hours of a day playing online or games against himself, and studying his cards (with their specific powers detailed in type too small for me to read).

It has occurred to me that this is a "latency period" activity par excellence. Sexuality, fleshy human interactions have been replaced by numbers (for the powers) and elaborate drawings and magical capacities and precise, inflexible rules. Particularly interesting is the fact that Jonah did not come to this latency activity until after having sprouted some signs of sexual maturity and becoming a little interested in girls, and they in him. It was not until he needed a refuge from sexuality that he found one.

And thus we may come back to my friend with "food issues." It was not until she was on her own, her son having gone off, that she needed restriction, protection—and to include when she moved to Paris and needed special protection from the sensual pleasures of French food and Latin culture. After splitting up with her son, many things formerly taken for granted were no longer possible precisely because many things, just playing most certainly included, had become possible. (I subsequently read an interview with Adam Phillips in which he talked about our fears of our appetites, our desires. "[T]he point of knowing oneself is to contain one's anxieties about appetite. . . . An appetite is fearful because it connects you with the world in very unpredictable ways.")

It will be interesting to see how I react when Jonah goes to college. I joke that I am going to follow him, as the future General Douglas MacArthur's mother followed her son to West Point, renting an apartment across the road so that, with the aid of a telescope, she could keep an eye on him. As it stands now, my plan seems rather to spend more time in Paris, eating bread and cheese, drinking wine, . . .

Meanwhile, before concluding the present piece, I will note that some readers may protest that my analysis of my friend is not only excessively judgmental; the judgments are wrong. The fact is, the protestors may say, this woman either long was or recently became *allergic* to gluten, for example, and it was only when her parenting work was largely done that she had the time and space to pay more attention to her own health. In my opinion, however, this analysis ends up at more or less the same point as my own analyses. Enjoying the company of her son and fully engaged and protected by this companionship—both from the desires of others and from some of her own strongest desires—she ate omnivorously. Once on her own, more vulnerable, she began to have trouble eating, trouble with foods, with living—be this as a result of recognizing her allergies, hers and others' desires, or some combination of all three.

These days I find myself thinking of the pillow forts that my first girlfriend and I built and got inside of and . . . just played. Life feels different when—instead of exposed, on your own—you are or can feel like a lucky child, with a rug and soft walls and a warm companion who may, like you, be a little awkward or silly, and who enjoys many of the same games as you. Living, and under-protected from external forces and from our feelings, thoughts and drives—this presents problems for many of us. Our children might do well to urge us to just play, to try, perhaps along with them, to rediscover just playing.

IV

Stealin', Stealin'

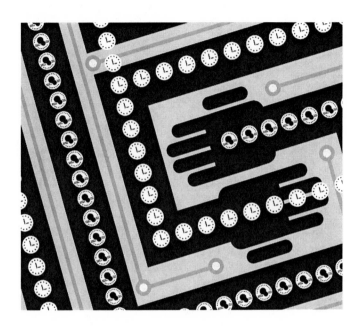

I'm stealin', stealin', pretty mama
Don't you tell on me
I'm stealin' back to my
Same old used to be

—American folk song first recorded by the Memphis
Jug Band, 1928

Stealin', Stealin'

M ay readers not have been misled either by the lines from the Memphis Jug Band song, or by your bank, cable company, newscasters and government officials, favorite entertainment products, . . . For years now my three guitars and two pianos have been gathering dust in my apartment. I no longer regularly read a newspaper either, nor do I regularly follow the news. If, however, I happen to see a copy of the *New York Times* business and sports section left out in a restaurant or at the Y, I will glance at the headlines and perhaps take the pages to read. It might be said that this section, with its stories about business and sports, continues to offer glimpses of contemporary life and human nature in languages that I can understand, that seem not to mislead.

The other week, on a Monday, the left-hand side of the first page offered commentary about a wealthy entrepreneur's attempt to use a management-led buyout to take private the company he served as chief executive. The second paragraph was a quote from a wealthy Wall Street investor: "Management-led buyouts are a giant case of inside trading by management against their own shareholders." Insider trading is of course an illegal activity—a form of stealin', we might call it—and the *Times* and other papers routinely feature stories about this or that wealthy company, financial whiz or monetarily ambitious young employee going on trial for insider trading.

It might be asked: Why read yet another story which simply reworks the tried-and-true plot of any number of previous stories? Is it like some people's taste for Hollywood movies or love songs, which also feature such reworking? That is, the pleasure lies in the familiarity, in being able to readily identify the good guys and the bad ones, and in knowing in advance what will happen to them?

The right-hand side of this particular business section had a story, one of several in the paper that day, about financial crisis in Cyprus, a temporary closing of the banks there and a proposed extraordinary levy on large deposits in the banks. As has been well known, and as the *Times* suggested in a subsequent article, Cyprus's economic model was built around financial services for foreigners seeking ways to dodge taxes and launder dirty money. And Cyprus is hardly the only economy to have been based on what has come to be called "offshore banking" (and this notwithstanding that landlocked nations such as Switzerland, Luxembourg and Andorra have been pioneers in the field).

My apologies to those readers who might still be expecting me to write something about the United States's more musical blues or about sports—about, say, my increasingly ghoulish fascination with the disappointing performance of one of my favorite sports teams. For the moment at least, that story seems to offer no moral beyond the one offered by many a sports season and in the disclaimers of investment documents: "past performance is no guarantee of future results." But again, are the business section stories more various? Laws and rules are honored in the breach; insiders take money from outsiders or from the public and its government, or with the cooperation of government officials who are financially rewarded for their cooperativeness. If and when some of the insiders get caught, they pay fines that are a small percentage of their ill-gotten gains, and some of them, typically lower-level operators, may do a little jail time. A government official may be disgraced. As has been remarked time and again, the penalties for getting caught committing low-dollar, lower-class crimes are much higher than for robbery done on a larger scale in the world of business.

Two days later I happened to pick up another iteration of this section of the *Times*. The lead story of the business section was about how "the nation's strongest bank" which "used to be known for carrying special sway with regulators . . . " What does this mean? That, on account of its strength, it used to get away with a lot of shady dealings? In any case, the story concerned how the bank stood currently accused of several instances of lying to investors and regulators and of misinforming some of its mortgage holders, to their detriment. Another story told how a hedge fund trader had agreed to pay the government more than $600 million "to settle accusations of insider trading," and how this fine was not affecting the trader's ability to continue in business or to buy famous art works. A story on the next page was about how another large bank had been faulted for "breakdowns in money laundering controls that threatened to allow tainted money to move through the United States."

A reader might be excused for concluding that all money, and perhaps the art works it acquired as well, was tainted. It should also be noted that there are fashions in news, just as with art, movies, music, clothes, books of essays. A big story breaks and somehow speaks to the *zeitgeist*, and the next thing you know the media finds many more similar stories and one may have the sense of a sort of epidemic. Bullying, for example, is an age-old (and horrible) practice, but the media has recently discovered that, as the saying goes, bullying has legs, and so we may get the sense that bullying is now extraordinarily widespread (which it probably is) and is now a problem as never before (which is likely not the case). And so, too, with stealing, insider trading, money laundering, tax avoidance, lying and misinformation by business leaders.

Would we say then that what has changed in recent years, in the wake of the global financial crisis, is what the media—or the center-left Establishment media?— reports? Before, the impression we were given, rightly or wrongly, was that business was basically an honest if highly competitive and money-obsessed undertaking. There were a few bad apples, a few low-lifers, used-car salesmen or shoddy war profiteers, but they were the exception, and certainly had not gone to the elite schools, did not work at the elite firms. Now the impression is that large businesses and business leaders are, like the Mafia and its dons, engaged in criminal activities on a large scale. The news stories referred to above involve four CEOs in particular. One of them went to the Wharton School of Business at the University of Pennsylvania, another to the Harvard Business School; one dropped out of the University of Texas at Austin, and the fourth graduated from Harvard College.

Some readers may object that these businesses and their

leaders are not *only* engaged in criminal activities, that ill-gotten gains account for less than half, perhaps much less than half, of their profits. This may be the case. But supposing that we were then left with the following alternative conclusion: Committing crimes, violating rules and regulations, engaging in deceit and helping others engage in it forms a part, large or small, of the standard successful business career. (See *Hosea*: "The merchant uses dishonest scales and loves to defraud.") In some cases, the fraudulent part may be relatively small, and in other cases—Cyprus's bankers, the hedge-fund trader willing to pay a $600 million fine to avoid more dire consequences, Bank of America paying a $16.65 billion fine, HSBC's laundering of billions for drug cartels and for banks with links to terrorist organizations—the criminal part may be rather larger. But in either case, be the take big or small, it would seem that business involves criminal activities. Proudhon's phrase was « La propriété, c'est le vol ! » (Property is theft.)

I do not read the sports section for the doping stories or for the stories about basketball or soccer referees in league with gambling interests. I have a little more interest in the stories about the business of college football and basketball, which basically involves insiders stealing from outsiders—from large numbers of lower-class youths hoping to become professional athletes and in fact already being professional athletes without getting paid professional wages. But sports is not (not yet?) the central activity of the United States. We may believe that sports stories point to larger ills—or virtues!—of our society, but we only occasionally decide that what is happening in the sports world should be our central concern. A few Americans go to college to play sports and make lots of money for the colleges, their coaches, the media and the athletic-equipment companies, but the "real education" they get is in exploitation, in the business of college sports. This is certainly a problem, many of us are prepared to say, but we would also say that there are larger problems with the American education system. On the one hand, a lot of students emerge from it heavily indebted but without sufficient skills or credentials to be successful in the current global economy. (Only a few have learned how to steal effectively, on a large scale?) On the other hand, even more students emerge without much perspective on themselves, the global economy and how they might be (or even just wish to be?) something more than a cog, or thief, in an economic machine.

"The business of America is business," President Coolidge is famously, if not quite accurately quoted as having said. Three years before the Memphis Jug Band released its reflections on the business of love, Coolidge, in a speech to the Society of American Newspaper Editors in January 1925, said:

> After all, the chief business of the American people is business. They are profoundly concerned with producing, buying, selling, investing and prospering in the world. I am strongly of the opinion that the great majority of people will always find these the moving impulses of our life.

From this perspective, the news that business—in the United States and elsewhere—is intimately connected with criminality, with violating the laws and regulations of the countries within which the business is done, this is a piece of information of some significance. Are we being led to conclude that we are a nation of thieves? Or is it just that we happen to be led by thieves, that financial power and all that goes along with it adheres to thieves? I find myself reminded that a large part of the wealth of Elizabethan England came from what Sir Francis Drake was able to steal from Spanish ships carrying gold and silver that had been, more or less, stolen from the "new world." And the early twenty-first century is hardly the first time we and our media noticed the prevalence of thievery among our business and financial leaders. The nineteenth century's "robber barons" come quickly to mind.

It is, however, relatively easy to read and write about things that happened long ago, but as regards the stealing going on now, my sense is that the news is simply too difficult to digest, and, as it also poses problems for the business operators themselves, it will not be long before this kind of news will fall out of fashion and out of our memories as well. (Coolidge also noted in his speech that the media are on one side purveyors of information and opinion and on the other side purely business enterprises.)

S tealin', stealin'. The song has been recorded many, many times over, to include by Bob Dylan, Jim Kweskin, Janis Joplin, the Grateful Dead. It's in our blood. There are those who would say we stole a whole continent.

Afterword

I would call attention to David Harvey's writing on the recent wave of "accumulation by dispossession." See his *The New Imperialism* (Oxford University Press, 2003), e.g. from page 147:

> Stock promotions, Ponzi schemes, structured asset destruction through inflation, asset-stripping through mergers and acquisitions, and the promotion of levels of debt incumbency that reduce whole populations, even in the advanced capitalist countries, to debt peonage, to say nothing of corporate fraud and dispossession of assets (the raiding of pension funds and their decimation by stock and corporate collapses) by credit and stock manipulations—all of these are central features of what contemporary capitalism is about. The collapse of Enron dispossessed many of their livelihoods and their pension rights. But above all we have to look at the speculative raiding carried out by hedge funds and other major institutions of finance capital as the cutting edge of accumulation by dispossession in recent times.

The famous phrase "Property is theft" comes from the opening lines of Pierre-Joseph Proudhon's *Qu'est-ce que la propriété ?*

> Si j'avais à répondre à la question suivante : Qu'est-ce que l'esclavage ? et . . .
>
> If I were asked to answer the following question: What

is slavery? and I should answer in one word—It is mur-
der!—my meaning would be understood at once. No
extended argument would be required . . . Why, then,
to this other question: What is property? may I not
likewise answer—It is robbery!—without the certainty
of being misunderstood? The second proposition is, after all, only a transformation of the first.

16

Sick

Sick, I went with Jonah, then two years old, to the drugstore in the village where we had a weekend house. This particular drugstore was a link in one of the several drugstore chains that around this time were accused of aggressively lobbying their customers to switch from cheaper versions of drugs that their doctors had prescribed to more expensive ones that were not necessarily as effective. As I recall, for these lobbying efforts the drugstores were being paid by drug companies, and in some cases customers' prescriptions were being changed without the customers' or their doctors' prior knowledge or approval. But let us proceed as if such matters were beside the point.

At this store, as in most stores to which young children are taken, certain products—little games, candies, brightly colored packages of stickers, cards featuring pictures of animals—were displayed at the eye and hand levels of young children. As I was waiting for my prescription to be filled, Jonah, as many a child will, began pulling some of these products off the shelves. The chance of his making a mess was good, as was the possibility of his damaging some of the packaging. And, as the store was hoping he would, Jonah asked if we might buy some of these so attractive things.

American parents have stock phrases for rejecting such requests—"You don't really want that"; "Put that back where you found it." We also have principles and cautionary sayings: a child should not make a mess of things that do not belong to him; "You break it, you bought it." We also give in to our children's demands. Not always, perhaps just on those days when the child is particularly charming or cranky or sick, or when we are sick or in a hurry or ebullient or distracted. We buy the bauble or candy. "I'll buy you this one, but that's it." The store has its sale—at times more than one.

The combination of American mores with stores' relentless solicitation of children can make going shopping with young children annoying, both for the parents and for other shoppers who must listen to and be delayed by the parents and children's squabbling. And there is the energy consumed in trying to control one's child, the reminder that one's financial resources have their limits. When one relents and buys something one did not want to buy, there is first the additional expense, and then the additional annoyance when one sees that one's child is at best temporarily mollified. As a rule the item is so unengaging, the candy so unnourishing, that the child is almost immediately hungry again, wanting to buy more.

Sick, it occurred to me that day in the drugstore that I had no obligation to a store that was forcing my child and me into conflict, trying to use my child to badger me into spending money I did not want to spend on products I did not want to buy, products that were not in any sense good for him. Rather than consuming my energy trying to restrain my son from making a mess of the store and such of its products as he could reach, I could hope that, if Jonah really went wild, his behavior would encourage this store and perhaps others like it to stop trying to seduce little children. Would this were a reasonable response to contemporary commercial savagery.

But such thinking is more entertaining than anything else. However annoying or absurd a situation may be, most of us try to behave and get our children to behave like the other "nice" people around us do. We are anxious to fit in and to help our children fit in, to feel part of a community and perhaps even to gain status within it. Beyond conforming or ladder-climbing, beyond the sake of appearances more generally, we may not see any other sense or goodness in behaving the way our fellow citizens behave. We may feel that many of our fellow citizens have confused custom and conventional ideas of "good behavior" with virtue or some larger moral truth. But again, we understand that if we and our children do not follow the rules, we may get a bad reputation, be scorned or ignored.

One exception must be noted, however, and to note it I will temporarily slip back to ancient Greece and the word ὕβρις (hubris). According to the classicist Cedric Whitman, the word originally meant assault and battery, and it never quite lost the overtones of physical violence, even when, during the classical period, the word came to be used to describe the arrogance of the rich and mighty. The classicist Kenneth Dover writes that the term came to be applied

> to any kind of behavior in which one treats other people just as one pleases, with an arrogant confidence that one will escape paying any penalty for violating their rights and disobeying any law or moral rule accepted by society, whether or not such a law or rule is regarded as resting ultimately on divine sanctions.

In the United States, not all but some hubristic people ("sociopaths" is a current word) become rich and powerful in part through ignoring community standards and treating other people as means to their personal ends. Subsequently such people may seek to rehabilitate their reputations or provide cover for ongoing reprehensible business practices by donating to charity a portion of their brazenly gotten gains. Gossip about these individuals' brazenness also becomes one of the ways that the individuals' status is recognized and valued. To be rich or powerful is not to have to play by the rules; to be blatantly not playing by the rules suggests power or wealth. Or, to elaborate on what the Canadian philosopher Charles Taylor has said in regards to our political system, an ambitious American does not seek to be a part of the system, either as a ruler or as a subject. He or she seeks to manipulate the system for his or her own ends, and thus to feel and appear superior to the many lesser souls who do participate and are manipulated.

If, however, those of us who are not so hubristic or rich, we of the dwindling middle and burgeoning lower classes—if we let our children treat stores' merchandise in the same uncaring manner that stores treat us (us adults and us children), we will likely find ourselves scorned by other members of our communities. (Interestingly, the scorn might be for acting in an inferior, not "well brought up" manner, or for acting uppity, as if we were richer, more powerful, more well-born than we are.)

As regards the small town in which I found myself sick and shopping—an old farming town that was now a bit of a suburb and a bit of a weekend retreat—it might have been only the longtime big-city residents, the weekend-retreaters such as myself, who would even consider letting one of their children run amok in a store. In a big city, should a store or group of people find one's behavior objectionable, there is always another store or group a few blocks away, and there is little chance that people at the next locations will have heard about one's behavior elsewhere. But in a small town most everybody hears about most everything out of the ordinary that anyone else has done, and gossips are busy inventing things to snicker about. (My big-city workplace is at least equally catty, and for much the same reason: little people scrambling to feel a little superior or to raise themselves a rung or two, or a seeming rung or two, above others.)

A parent has a great, if not entirely fulfillable responsibility to prepare his child to survive as well as possible in the social, professional, commercial and psychological jungles in which the child will find herself. And learning must be done step-by-step. Even if a child is ready intellectually to understand a complex moral argument, if she lacks a sufficient foundation of experience it will be an academic concept, hard to take seriously or retain.

In *The Education* Henry Adams recalls how as a young man he asked the veteran New York politician Thurlow Weed if he thought that no politician could be trusted. "Mr. Weed hesitated for a moment," Adams writes, "then said in his mild manner:—'I never advise a young man to begin by thinking so.'"

May each parent decide for himself at what age his child is ready to move on from "Put that back where you found it" to "Americans think that if you are not going to buy an item you should put it back where you found it," or, "The store has suckered you into grabbing that item, now do you want to let it sucker us into giving them money for it?" Or, "If you think anyone may have seen you break that item and you want to fit in, it may make sense for you now to make a show of telling some member of the store staff what you did and that you want to pay for the item."

Or perhaps the task is much more straightforward: devote all one's efforts to ensuring that one's children have sufficient wealth, power and lack of empathy so that the rules do not apply to them. I would be sad if Jonah did not learn to recognize others—and hardly just humans, all beings, animal, vegetable and mineral—as ends in themselves. But I am not so sick as to fail to see that the world is dominated by the hubristic, their thieving drugstore chains included. I think he has some special gifts, my son. May one of them be finding a way to survive, even thrive.

17

Ethics of our twenty-first century

1   I had worked out at a Y, not my regular Y, and was taking my watch and wallet out of a locked box on the wall. A man I did not know, a man in his 50s, came up to me, seemingly to warn me about there being robbers in the men's locker room. He himself had been robbed, he said. However, he soon added that he had made $800 as a result. The thief had taken only his credit cards, and he, the putative victim, had called his credit-card companies and cancelled the cards, thereby absolving himself from responsibility for any charges that might be or had been made on them by the thief. And it so happened that the day of the theft was a day when he had gone to a department store and charged $800, and the credit-card companies' computer systems had not taken this into consideration. That is, any card purchases from the day of the theft forward were not billed to him, and this included the $800 he had spent.

I am assuming that the theft had not been dreamed up by the man as a way of trying to get out of paying for his purchases. But I have wondered—Wouldn't a locker-room robber quickly grab a whole wallet, any cash included, rather than taking the time and trouble to pick out the credit cards? I have begun to think it axiomatic: any story once examined will reveal itself to be a work of fiction, or an expression of inner workings of the storyteller's mind.

Nonetheless, accepting the man's story on its face, I am prepared to say that most Americans of all types and ages, myself included, would have responded to this supposed stroke of good fortune as the man had done. That is, he did nothing; he did not call the credit-card companies again to report the mistake and make himself again liable for the $800 he had spent. One might say that the man was, therefore, guilty of stealing.

Why do we not then condemn the man's behavior, and why

are we willing to admit that we would have acted (or not acted) as he did? For one, we make a distinction between sins of omission and commission. If the companies had called the man and asked him if the $800 in purchases had been made by him, we might blame him if he lied and said no, but in the present case all he did was keep his mouth shut, not pick up the phone again. Moreover, experience has taught us that picking up the phone and calling a credit-card company (or cable TV company, airline, bank, . . .) is no simple matter. There will be the automatic voice and all her commands to get past. (We are doing companies' record-keeping work for them and without compensation.) There will be time on hold, and it may be necessary to explain and re-explain, and at some length, what happened. And, in the end, the chances that the matter will be successfully, accurately resolved are not high.

More than all this, however, when I present people with this ethical dilemma, the first thing they say is that the credit-card companies themselves are thieves. If you believe that a company is routinely stealing money from you and millions of other people, why would you bother calling them to help them steal a little less?

Several caves for energetic spelunking now beckon, but we are only going to peek into two of their mouths before moving on to the next ethical dilemma. One of these caves contains the fact that many business activities involve theft or similar disreputable activities of one kind of another, some of them legal and many of them illegal but carried out anyway by large and so-called reputable businesses. The large-scale money laundering carried out by the HSBC bank comes to mind as does the thievery of my landlords, who mixed illegally overcharging thousands of tenants with sitting on the boards of prominent civic institutions. They sat on these boards and gave to charities at least in part so that their daily thievery would go unpunished.

Further, many of us work for drug companies, banks, landlords, credit-card companies and the like. We participate wittingly or unwittingly in the thievery and have a front-row seat for observing it, and this even as we are also victimized by other businesses and perhaps also by our own employers. (See, for example, the many employees who have had their pension funds raided or insufficiently funded by their companies' owners, or the many employees who are not paid the overtime wages to which they are legally entitled, or cab drivers cheated of their tips by fleet owners.) So, among many other things, it is interesting to me that we have a way of deciding that certain specific companies or industries are particularly reprehensible, and that we rarely move from there to making generalizations about the economic system in which we find ourselves caught. (See, again, Proudhon, "Property is theft," or Marx on *Geld* (money): "I am an evil, dishonest, conscienceless, brainless man; but money is honored, and therefore so is its possessor.")

I have also always made one very large exception to the keep-what-you-get moral code sketched above. If I like a person or institution that I am dealing with, and no matter how poorly I may in fact know them, however new our acquaintance may be, I will go out of my way to be honest with them—for example, to point out that they have given me too much change or forgotten to charge me for something, no matter how expensive this item may be. And, by contrast, if I have formed a negative impression of a person or institution, to include if I sense that they have tried or are trying to steal from me either directly or through the more subtle mechanisms of business, I will take advantage of such opportunities as present themselves to cheat them right back, even to try to take more from them than they have managed to take from me.

Of course I also have a weather eye out for not being arrested, and, as it so happens, the only time I was ever arrested was back in 10th grade, when I was arrested for doing something (chopping down highway advertising billboards in order to beautify the roadways) that I had *not* done. "Nicely," the reason I was arrested was because at that time (1969) the police—fighting a somewhat secret war against the Anti-War Movement and thus against the First Amendment as well—were paying some of my fellow high school students to spy on and inform against those of us who were politically active and leftwing. It is also axiomatic that if the process is corrupt, the information it produces will be too.

We would like to think that in my case some young, high-school spy simply made a mistake. But the information that has subsequently come out about the FBI'S counter-intelligence program COINTELPRO suggests that this "mistake" was, rather, par for the course. In the Fifties and Sixties the FBI apparently worked with police forces to deliberately give false testimony and present fabricated evidence as a pretext for false arrests and wrongful imprisonment of people whose political views and goals ran counter to their own. US law-enforcement officials conducted illegal break-ins, committed acts of vandalism, assaults, beatings . . . And then there is the other side of this coin: the law-enforcement officers and friends of those in power who continue to be allowed to commit with impunity more purely self-interested crimes. Sometimes these crimes involve running red lights or driving drunk. Sometimes they involve small sums of money; sometimes very large ones. As Lewis Mumford wrote of the "robber barons" of our late nineteenth century:

> [T]he concentration of great fortunes, built up by graft, speculation, war-profits, or the outright dona-tion of priceless lands to great railway corporations, acquisitions which were not called theft, and doles which were not denounced . . . only because the sums involved were so huge and the recipients so rich.

In such a welter, what do we make of the guy at the YMCA who let his credit-card company pay for his department-store spree?

The second cave mouth to peek into: When the stranger at the Y told me this story, he was telling this story to a stranger (me), and apparently without appreciating the not necessarily attractive light the story shed on him. Among other things, I could not help feeling there was a racist undertone to his story. One thing he, a white man, was telling me was to be careful, there were robbers at the Y, and while he did not explicitly name the race of the people he suspected of breaking into his and other people's lockers, I—perhaps this is *my* racism—got the impression he was referring to young black men. Later I found myself wondering: Supposing the thief, no matter his color, had used the credit cards to buy food for his family, whereas "the victim" had used the cards to get for himself (with the credit-card companies' money, as it turned out) a larger flat-screen TV: Who would have been the greater thief? One might have sinned by commission, breaking into a locker, and the other by omission, not calling a credit-card company, but both ended up with things (foods and TV) that did not properly belong to them? Or that less properly belonged to them than did the $800 to the credit-card companies? We might ask, too, who had been harmed by all these crimes or by this sequence of events? Stockholders?

Why tell the story to anyone, and why to a stranger, why to me? In retrospect my sense is that it was precisely the man's uneasiness about his behavior that had led him to try the story out on a stranger. Why me? Because I was about his age and skin color (pale)? Because there was that intangible something in my appearance that suggested I would listen dispassionately, without voicing any judgments?

My point here is that while there is a social consensus— the man had not done wrong to not have paid for his credit- card purchases—still this conflicts with another value or values which parents, teachers and others downloaded into our brains without first asking our permission. This might be the value of honesty, of not stealing, or it might be a more sophisticated "value," which encourages us to distinguish between "them"— the lower classes, young black men, or thieving millionaires and billionaires, drug-company executives and members of Congress and of our state legislatures—and "us," respectable members of the middle class. We may not be rich—we are going to the Y, after all (and perhaps happy to go there!)—but we have principles, principles that we live by, principles that are not entirely self-serving or opportunistic.

If I steal $800 from a credit-card company, or from its millions of shareholders (of whom I am probably one, via this or that mutual fund of which I hold a few shares), the most significant effect is on my sense of myself. At least insofar as memories of my action remain in my consciousness or subconsciousness, it will be with some difficulty that I can think of myself as an honest person. I do not consider this an entirely bad thing. Nietzsche proposed, "When virtue has slept, she will wake up more refreshed." I would say rather that in moments of coming up short and realizing we have come up short there are opportunities to get to know ourselves better and to soften our criticism of others.

In any case, I do think that this was what the stranger at the Y was really talking to me about—not about these other robbers I should watch out for and not about his good fortune, the $800 worth of free stuff, but about himself and his sense of himself. And, perhaps, as I shall now discuss, the man was also touching on an unsettling aspect of this brave new world in which we live.

2   As I began writing about this incident and another one, still to come, I recalled an incident from my youth, an incident in which I was the sinner of omission, or the beneficiary of a tiny bit of luck, the recipient of a few extra groceries I did not really want. A college student temporarily back home, I had driven some distance from my parents' house to a suburban supermarket to do the weekly shopping for the family. This supermarket had a system whereby after the bags were packed they were put on a conveyor belt, and young men loaded the bags from the back of the belt into shoppers' cars. As I recall, numbers were written on the paper bags with a grease pencil. So I pulled up in front of the store, popped the trunk, showed my number—19, let's say—and the young men loaded all the bags with 19s on them into my car and closed the trunk, and I drove away.

In another twenty minutes or so I was home, and I discovered that not only did I have my half a dozen bags of groceries, I also had several bags belonging to someone else. This being another person's groceries, the items and brands did not accord with my families' tastes and habits. The noodles were not the brand we bought, and I remember my parents objecting in particular to a box of Pepperidge Farm croutons, an item which would be beneath us to consume. (We made our own croutons.)

There was a question in our kitchen: Didn't I think I should take the other person's groceries back to the store? No, I did not think so. I was interested in dinner. The store itself had put someone else's groceries in the car. Let the store deal with its mistake and with the customer, who was going to be inconvenienced and irate no matter what I now did. Likely by the time I got back to the supermarket, the other customer would already be yelling at the manager or shopping all over again.

Writing this all out here, I do not feel I should have any great ethical concerns about the decision that I made, and which my parents went along with. (After all, one of them could have driven the alien groceries back to the supermarket. We would have saved some dinner for Mom or Dad.) And yet, why has this little incident stayed in my conscious memory, and for more than three decades now? Is it a gnawing sense of having done wrong, or of not having done right? (My story and the $800 man's also point up how our ethical thinking is simply outdated, it reflects a time when relations between people were more personal and direct—e.g. buyers and sellers confronting one another in a town market. Nowadays, a company's computer may erroneously charge you $800, and it may take more than $800 of your time to get the mistake corrected.) In New York I am routinely cheated by taxi drivers and in food stores where it can be hard to know the prices of items or to clearly see the weights and prices being rung up on the cash register. (And this in violation of various laws that address such chicanery.) I used to complain, vocally and in writing, about defective products, bad service, bad food served to me in restaurants, but in late middle-age I have had a little success with teaching myself not to worry about any of this, so long as the sums are small or smaller than the value of the time I would need to invest in order to get treated more fairly. And, on the other hand—and this has been a consistent policy throughout my life—if money or goods that are not mine, or have not previously been mine, happen to fall into my lap, I keep them. (I note the saying "Possession is nine-tenths of the law.")

3   The seeds of this essay were sown in a taxi cab, riding home from a middle-school skating party with a friend of Jonah's. This boy, 13 years old, told about how he had recently been walking along a sidewalk with his mother and somewhere ahead of them an elderly woman was walking. All of a sudden the wind or a more complex set of events caused some bills to blow out of the old lady's purse toward him. He gathered up the bills, realizing that the total was $300, all of which he brought straight away to the old lady. It seems, however, that she neglected either to thank him or to give him a reward, or both. The boy told me that his mother then remarked that, given the old lady's response, or lack of response, "you should have just kept the money." It is not that she was counseling her son to do otherwise than he had done. From one perspective, it could be she imagined she was teaching a version of the moral principle I touched on above. If you have a good impression of another person, or at least not a bad impression, then you indeed should treat her and him with a certain kindness and generosity—in a neighborly fashion, we might call this, while recognizing that neighbors are not always treated nicely, nor always nice.

At the same time, I felt there was something avaricious in the mother's comment, as if it had not been just a matter of a warm "thank you!" but of a reward. At issue was $300. If the boy had not returned it, the older woman was out $300, so what was it worth to her to get the money back? $10? $50? $299.99? (Jonah, who was also in the taxi, agrees that his friend's mother thought the older woman should have offered a reward, and Jonah thinks $20 would have been the right amount.) I noted that the boy's family belonged to the business class, his father worked in investment banking. From this perspective, perhaps the incident was, let's call it, amoral—i.e. outside the realm of morality. It was a business transaction. How much is it worth to you to get back what once was your $300? How much is it worth to credit-card companies to get their customers to tell them when mistakes have been made in these customers' favor? My being falsely arrested cost my family a certain amount of money in legal fees. How much would we have been willing to pay the police, in advance, to leave us alone? Every year when a policeman calls asking me to donate to the Police Athletic League I have the sense that this is the subtext: A little contribution and perhaps a sticker for my car's bumper (not that I have a car) could be well worth it to me, and I'd be helping athletic kids besides.

4   This piece began as a series of "ethical dilemmas," featuring questions of the "how would you behave if?" sort. It has not slipped far from that original mooring. In the beginning I had a vague idea that the ethical-dilemmas approach might be of interest to students about Jonah's age, and so I asked Jonah to read the first draft of this text. There proved to be something right about my instinct. Walking across town the next day I walked right through the middle of a group that was blocking the sidewalk in order to take pictures of themselves. Jonah felt that my behavior, which was intentional, was wrong. There had been a better alternative: walking around the group, which was what he had done. I proposed that a person has no obligation to not inconvenience strangers who are already acting in a way that inconveniences people who are strangers to them. Jonah disagreed, proposing that if it is easy for you to be nice to other people, and even if they have not been nice to you, you should be nice. He did not articulate why you should do this, but perhaps it has to do with the Golden Rule or setting an example for others or holding oneself to a higher standard, and even as one recognizes that most people do not live up to this standard. I raised the problem that if you are nicer to people than they are to you, this may degrade you in their eyes and encourage them to continue to treat you badly, or yet worse. (Recently a boy at Jonah's school had kicked Jonah out of a lunchtime poker game. The boy does not himself play in the game; he seems a bit afraid to compete; but he brings the cards and chips and plays at controlling who is allowed to play and who is not. Jonah, caught up in this other, non-poker game, had—rather than simply scorning this manipulative boy and playing with other friends—tried to get back in the game-master's good graces. A losing strategy, I had felt.)

Meanwhile I count myself very lucky to have a Jonah, and this particular Jonah, with whom to discuss ethics. Toward the end of the discussion, I recounted for him the ethical dilemmas presented in another of my essays ("It was a warm, sunny day"). In this case Jonah was quite firm in his evaluation of my refusal to take a picture for a tourist who had previously—obtusely if unwittingly— disturbed me as I was trying to get some writing done. Jonah insisted repeatedly that I had acted "like a 5 year old." I begged, and continue to beg, to differ (and without wishing to underestimate the capacities of 5 year olds!). As I have written elsewhere, one of the foundations of my ethics is—in addition to the overarching value of talking and just being with Jonah—an extension of an idea of Kant's, from his *Grundlegung zur Metaphysik der Sitten* (*Fundamental Principles of the Metaphysic of Morals*). And I would insist that for me at least this is an emotional, rather than rational foundation. Every being is an end in itself, and is entitled to be treated as such. His, her or its nature and aims, or lack thereof, are deserving of an equal level of consideration and respect. You might say, however, that I believe this with a vengeance. The person who treats other human beings, or animals or plants, natural resources, etc., as merely *serviable* (as available and recognizable only for their ability or lack of ability to help "me" or "us"), such a person is still entitled to respect (as an end in herself or himself), but not to any kindness. Does this find me caught, as it were, midway between the apostle Peter's "honor all" and the Old Testament's eye for an eye? Purity in ethics is an ideal that disguises many realities.

18

My bar mitzvah (and Thanksgiving) speech

For James and Jonah, as they are called to participate
in a minyan or as citizens of these United States

While I was never bar mitzvahed, I have learned that the bar mitzvah boy is given a passage of the Torah to study, and that he, 13 years old, gives a speech at his family's synagogue about the meaning of his Torah portion. (This usually involves claiming to have learned something about being a good person.) My text was given to me by PBS, but perhaps also by God in a certain sense, one evening during my fifty-ninth year. The text took the form of a documentary about the dancer and choreographer Jerome Robbins.

One November Friday night, an evening before attending the bar mitzvah of a friend of Jonah's, I was, for other reasons, quite tired, and I lay down on my couch a little after 8, clicker in hand. At 9 this documentary came on. Previously I knew very little about Robbins, and I have not been a particular fan of Broadway musicals or of the American Ballet Theatre. It is possible that, except for clips on TV and a remake of his first ballet, "Fancy Free," I have never seen a Robbins production, and if I have now watched a two-hour documentary, . . . I am like a tourist who briefly visited a foreign city.

Two things struck me. One was how dedicated Robbins was to his chosen crafts: dance and choreography. For 60 years he just kept working and working, always trying to learn, always trying to get it right. This level and consistency of dedication is in and of itself extraordinary, a kind of genius independent of whatever creative and expressive talents one may also have. Secondly, the major event of Robbins's life occurred on quite another stage, when he agreed to testify to the House Committee on Un-American Activities (HUAC) and during his testimony he "named names": four people who, he said, had been communists, as he in his youth had been. In doing this he destroyed these four people's careers for some period of years and turned them into pariahs. In the documentary one of the named says that for three months she and her husband did not receive a single phone call. Her friends were all afraid of themselves being caught, condemned, unable to get work.

One of the subtexts of this portion of the documentary was the anti-Semitism of the communist-hunting of the McCarthy period. I have subsequently read in Wikipedia that the reason Senator McCarthy hired a Jew, Roy Cohn, as his chief counsel, choosing him over another eager applicant, Robert Kennedy, was "reportedly in part to avoid accusations of an anti-Semitic motivation" for his Senate subcommittee's investigations. And it is not for nothing that McCarthy and his great supporter Joseph Kennedy were Irish Catholics, anxious to be fully accepted in a country in which Catholics were a minority and the Irish considered by many to be good for nothing but manual labor and police work. The "Red Scare" of the 1940s and '50s offered them an opportunity: Catholics could fit in by identifying Jews as the real outsiders.

Ostensibly McCarthy and the HUAC investigators who proceeded him were uncovering Americans who had, typically in their youth and during the Depression, been members of the American Communist Party. But HUAC's focus happened to be on the entertainment industry, a business dominated by Jews, some of whom were trying to build strong, independent labor unions that could win higher wages for professional, artistic and technical staff in the entertainment industry. The overt statement of the witch-hunts was that Americans who would join a Communist Party were not real Americans, and this both because the Communist Party had strong ties to the Soviet Union and because communism's ideology (e.g. "from each according to his ability, to each according to his need"?) challenged the American ("every man for himself"?) way. There was, however, another, less explicit statement: Jews were not Americans. This aspect of McCarthyism echoed the early days of Nazi rule during which Hitler's government, backed and advised by leading German bankers and industrialists, whipped up anti-

Semitic sentiments as a way of destroying the power of the labor unions and driving down wages. In the American case, xenophobia was whipped up and used to attack leftist Jews, not least those active in labor unions.

As I understand the history, there was a series of battles in the movie industry between the workers and the studio bosses, and some of the most significant of these battles were between, on the one hand, a set of unions (the IATSE or IA) that were controlled by the Mob in collusion with the studio bosses; and, on the other hand, a more democratic body, the CSU. The fundamental issues were control over the unions and workers and keeping down or raising wages. However, the Mob leaders and bosses came up with the idea of accusing their opponents of being communists—i.e. un-American, traitors. For example, in 1941 a movie producer named Walt Disney took out an ad in *Variety*, the Hollywood trade magazine, declaring his conviction that "Communist agitation" was behind a cartoonists and animators' strike going on at that time.

Such tactics proved so successful that anti-labor and anti-Semitic politicians in Washington and elsewhere adopted them. Thus the sad irony: Americans thought the goal, right or wrong, was rooting out communists, but this was only a means for controlling workers and keeping down wages—the wages of the vast majority of Americans, however anti-communist or anti-Semitic they may have been. (Variations on this tactic have been used over and over again, and the vast majority of Americans continue to be fooled by it and to lose track of who is fighting for their interests and who against them.)

The documentary's position was that the Jewish Robbins (née Rabinowitz) got caught during the McCarthy period because, like many a child of immigrants, he wanted nothing so much as to be accepted by his country, to fit in, to be liked not only for who he was but also because there was nothing he wanted more than to be a real American. (Which would be to say as unscrupulous as Walt Disney, Roy Cohn and Joseph Kennedy?) Myself, I have always felt that I belonged, that I was completely American, whether I liked it or not, and notwithstanding all my objections to American values, customs and politics. It is also the case that I am, as the Nazis would say, *Mischling*, a hybrid. (As most Americans and likely most "Aryan" Germans as well are, though the elements of the mix vary from family to family.) In my particular case, when my mother, from a Jewish family, announced to her father that she wanted to marry a man named Sam, her father joked that this Sam couldn't be Jewish because in those days no American Jews had Old Testament names. Boys from Jewish families were named Jack, Walt, Jerry, etc. to help them fit in, and making it clear to all, the boys included, that fitting in was the first priority. My mother also belongs to a very particular linguistic grouping in the United States: Children who grew up in Brooklyn but during their adolescence unlearned their Brooklyn accents, a bit as Liza Doolittle unlearned hers. As a result my mother has at times been mistaken for a foreigner, for someone who learned English very well but later in life. And it might be said that this approach to being an American was passed along to me. I learned French in adulthood and came to speak French with my wife and son in our home. As a result, sometimes when people hear me speak English they wonder what foreign country I come from. In fact, I can tell them with a smile, one of my ancestors was Priscilla (Mullins) Alden, one of the famous lovers of the Mayflower. My namesake, William Eaton, was the first American general to lead an imperialist army abroad, in North Africa, against the Barbary pirates: "To the shores of Tripoli; . . . First to fight for right and freedom, and to keep our honor clean," as the "Marines' Hymn" describes my ancestor's adventure.

Again, I take this to be not only my particular story, but also just one variation on the story of so many of us. A few days after the bar mitzvah I had dinner with a Brazilian-born friend who ended up outlining on the paper table-covering her family history. There was a Jewish grandmother whose family had come to Brazil to escape the Inquisition, but whose members were still, five centuries later, not considered real Brazilians, not even by some of the family members themselves. This concept of real "Brazilian" seemed reserved not for descendants of the people who occupied the land before it was conquered by Europeans, but for Europeans who were Catholics. Thus my friend also told me of a grandfather, the man who married her Jewish grandmother. He came from Germany in the 1920s and fit right in. He was, or claimed to be, Catholic. So many years later, growing up in suburban New Jersey, my friend's American-born son had insisted that for Thanksgiving his mother make *not* Brazilian food but rather both turkey and ham, to help him prove to the world and to himself that he was both American and not Jewish.

Robbins faced a second problem when it came to fitting in. He was a homosexual, and somewhat before the gay pride movement. He was a homosexual, and he was being hounded by FBI Director J. Edgar Hoover, who has since been thought to have been a homosexual and/or cross-dresser. According to the documentary, Hoover's agent in all this was the TV personality Ed Sullivan who persisted in threatening Robbins that, if he did not testify, his homosexuality would be exposed. I now regret every minute my sisters and I spent watching Sullivan's TV show when we were growing up. To not have the courage and autonomy to refuse to name names is one thing; to be forcing people to testify, and to be threatening to expose their sexual proclivities if they did not testify, this is both criminal and obscene. I am also sure that Sullivan's viciousness can be found in his programs, and Robbins's anxieties and self-centeredness in his dances, and that Disney's willingness to resort to slander as a way of making more money is there in his cartoons, and . . . And I am sure that through these widely viewed cultural products these "values," these ways of being and of being real Americans, have been passed along to many Americans, "impressionable youths" included.

According to the documentary (*Jerome Robbins: Something to Dance About*), Robbins was unwilling or unable to accept being outed as a homosexual because this would trash his immigrants' child's wish—to fit in. He may also have been afraid of not being able to get work. After being blacklisted, an up and coming Hollywood director named Abraham Polonsky directed only one more feature film in the remaining thirty years of his life. Robbins lived to work. To not have been able to work would have been torture. He went to Washington to testify and he named names. I have subsequently read, in a Joan Acocella piece in the *New* Yorker archives:

> [O]ther homosexual artists, such as Aaron Copland and Marc Blitzstein, stood firm . . . His [Robbins's] testimony makes shameful reading. He fell over himself to name names. As one congressman remarked gratefully, his level of coöperation was "a bit unusual."

The PBS documentary includes some commentary from a historian of the period. It is very difficult for those of us who were not living at that time and who were not in Robbins's shoes to condemn what he did, the historian says, and then, justly, I believe, he completes the thought: But, still, what Robbins did was both despicable and wrong. And in the larger scheme of things—and in Robbins's sensitive soul as well, the film suggested—this traitorous, cowardly action stayed in his mind longer than the pride he must also have felt given his extraordinary string of wildly popular dances and shows.

As the columnist Murray Kempton wrote some years ago:

> There come times when you have to go into capital, and be ready to face up to the loss of a lot, because you are wise enough to sense that the alternative is to lose everything. You will get through, and there will be a time to come when all that will be remembered about you is whether or not you gave the names.

I pause to note one irony, or several. This homosexual Jerome Robbins-Rabinowitz whose patriotism the US Congress challenged—in one of its shameful moments, though far from its only one—this Jerome Robbins-Rabinowitz, so afraid of not being accepted given who he in fact was—he has been, and perhaps as much as any American of his generation, responsible for giving Americans a way—an odd way?—of feeling proud of themselves. (I have in mind Robbins's direction or choreographing of such Broadway shows as *West Side Story, The King and I, Peter Pan* and *Fiddler on the Roof,* and of ballets like "Fancy Free" and "Dances at a Gathering.") Sometime after his testimony the State Department paid for Robbins and a group of dancers to tour Europe to show the world the greatness of American/"Free World" choreography. We might say, among other things, that freedom was something Robbins knew only in the breach. Even in his work he was, as we say, driven.

So now we come to the bar mitzvah. Not having been raised Jewish, I have attended services in a synagogue perhaps ten times in my whole life. Each time I attend a service, in addition to the beauty of the singing, I am struck by what my father might call the mumbo-jumbo (the clinging to ancient superstitions) of organized religion. The following wordings were not used at Jonah's friend James's bar mitzvah; I am here copying from a Reform Siddar (prayer book) I consulted subsequently:

> Exalted and hallowed be God's great name in the world which God created, according to plan. May the words of my mouth and the meditations of my heart be acceptable to You, Adonai, my Rock and my Redeemer.

While such prayers are being recited, I often find myself looking around the room at the other people, wondering if they really believe this stuff. At the bar mitzvah service for Jonah's friend, I found myself wondering if the rabbi even believed in God, or in anything like the God being described in the prayers he was leading. (Going back to anti-Vietnam-War days, my strongest religious connection has been to Quakerism, and above all to the power, often awful power, of Quaker meeting for worship. I taught "First Day School" when Jonah was little. I have read that 50 percent of Quakers do not believe in God. My own "God" is a kind of placeholder for the unknown and for the unknowable, and thus a reminder of the universe of human ignorance as well.)

Nevertheless, perhaps under the influence of the Robbins documentary I had watched the night before, or impressed by how proud James's parents were to have him going through this rite of passage and in front of all their relatives and friends—I appreciated a different aspect of the bar mitzvah service. It was as if there was another subtext, as if the "believers" there assembled were saying:

> We probably don't really believe these words we are say-
> ing, but we are saying them because this is what our
> ancestors have been saying for thousands of years. We
> are reaffirming this historical connection, and the con-
> nection is felt more strongly because in order to reaffirm
> it we are saying words whose superficial content we don't
> even bother thinking about. And we rejoice in saying
> these words, and we would say whatever is asked of us,
> because these are our people, this is our home.

As I sat in the synagogue I found myself thinking, too, of something I had read around the time of Yom Kippur, a few months earlier. In some German concentration camp a woman or group of women asked and were given permission to hold services. They had no rabbi and none of the ritual objects. They were starving and cold and disease-ridden and had seen so many die and expected to themselves die soon. They gathered together around a candle and sang the Kol Nidre, the haunting song of Yom Kippur. My thought, now, at this 2012 bar mitzvah in a well-to-do neighborhood of New York City, was that this, too, was why we say these time-worn prayers. Because over the course of thousands of years of human history, and in the future, periodically there have been and will be times when it will seem that all we have left to hold onto are our communal traditions, our imaginary Gods—and this even if we are also being made to suffer, being killed, for our beliefs or for our ethnic identification, persecuted and killed by our neighbors, invoking their gods. (Or killed in the interests of capital, or denied work so that wages can be driven down again.)

The French philosopher Henri Bergson, raised Jewish, is famous for, among other things, *not* having converted to Catholicism although he found himself drawn to it. In his last will, prepared in 1937, he wrote:

> Je me serais converti si je n'avais vu se préparer depuis
> des années . . . la formidable vague d'antisémitisme qui
> va déferler sur le monde. J'ai voulu rester parmi ceux
> qui seront demain des persécutés.

> I would have converted [to Catholicism] had I not seen
> the tremendous wave of anti-Semitism building over many
> years and now soon to break upon the world. I wanted to
> remain among those who tomorrow will be persecuted.

This to me comes closest to expressing my own Judaism, and my own Puritanism as well. If people are going to persecute and be persecuted for their beliefs, I will be among the persecuted. I may or may not have a choice in this, but I know my role, where I belong, where I will feel most at home.

In coming back toward Robbins's testimony to HUAC, I will pause for a moment on the Jewish rite of circumcision. Male individuals have a part of their anatomies, an intimate, sensitive part, taken away by their families and communities and before they are old enough to be consulted or say a word in their own defense. Personally I find this practice barbaric, and I refused to allow Jonah to be circumcised and notwithstanding the fact that current medical practice now has most every American boy being circumcised, usually before he leaves his first hospital, and with the doctor and hospital being handsomely rewarded for their pains.

I recently heard a young female American comedian making fun of uncircumcised penises and how disgusting they were. This linked with making fun of the French and their un-American accents. My position remains that, if for religious or health reasons my Jonah (or another boy) wants to have a piece of his penis cut off when he is older—or if he wants to do this in order not to be made fun of or thought disgusting—let this be his decision.

But penile circumcision is just one of the many forms of circumcision—or of invasions of privacy and autonomy—carried out by *homo sapiens* in the name of community. In parts of Spain, I believe, it is traditional during wedding ceremonies for the guests to cut off pieces of the groom's tie. And there are traditions of bloody wedding night sheets being thrown out to the guests to confirm the taking or sacrifice of the bride's virginity. In Russia and other cultures a new male colleague or visitor is not trusted until he gets drunk (very drunk) or otherwise inebriated with the established group. This is another tradition that I, not a drinker, do not like, but I understand it. Once drunk one makes confessions and says and does stupid things. The community now has something to hold over you and so can trust you. (For instance, if you confess to being a homosexual or to having had some homosexual experiences, this can be used as and when necessary to force you to testify or to betray a labor movement.)

When Robbins agreed to sacrifice himself—his autonomy and his honor—before the House Committee on Un-American Activities, he was showing the Congress and Americans as a whole that he was one of them. He probably knew that one of the chief communist-hunters, Roy Cohn, was also a homosexual, and he may have understood that the people taking, recording and listening to his testimony in the HUAC hearing room had plenty of secrets of one kind or another in their closets, and had also at key moments in their lives agreed to sacrifice their own integrity and to do shameful things in order to fit in—be it to not be ostracized in high school, to get or keep a job, to marry "well," become "partner" or get tenure or win election to Congress. This, we might say, is one of the ways in which communities are made, by demanding and overseeing the sacrifice of the autonomy—and with it some of the dignity—of the community members. (It is not for nothing that Jonah and his classmates put on ties—cords around their necks—to come to their friend James's bar mitzvah service. And since Jonah as yet does not know how to make the noose, I first made it around my own neck and then slipped it off my head and on to his. And his Belgian mother, watching, complained for him about his having to button the top button of his shirt—restricting breathing and freedom of movement. And I also saw some pride in Jonah's eyes, to be wearing a button-down shirt and tie like his dad.)

The shameful things we do in order to fit in—and in marking others to be ostracized so that we ourselves might be accepted—haunt us throughout our lives. In 1963, a namer of names, actor Sterling Hayden, declared, "I was a rat, a stoolie, and the names I named of those close friends were blacklisted and deprived of their livelihood." According to scholars Paul Buhle and Dave Wagner, Hayden "was widely believed to have drunk himself into a near-suicidal depression decades before his 1986 death." In the large organization where I earn my living, I daily work with people—straight and gay and of most every nationality and religious persuasion—who behave in Haydenesque fashion, badmouthing their colleagues (or identifying them rightly or wrongly as Jewish or otherwise abnormal) whenever an opportunity presents itself. This is how these quite ordinary people try to fit in and get ahead. And, yes, sadly, many of these badmouthers and ostracizers are people who, on account of their sexuality or for other reasons (including alcoholism, lack of interest in their jobs or lack of ability), feel themselves vulnerable to themselves being ostracized and discriminated against.

Myself, I remember once, I must have been about 18 years old, I was travelling with three people: my best male friend, a girl I was romantically, sexually interested in, and a girl who was, as the saying goes, just a friend, and Jewish besides, as the other two people were not. We all ended up in one big bed, and I played the lead role in communicating to this girl, the Jewish girl, that she was not wanted there, she should go sleep by herself while the other three of us stayed together. In the course of coming of age (and throughout adulthood) one has hundreds if not thousands of opportunities to behave in this way, and I am sure that this was not the only time that I was an ostracizer, though this is the incident that continues to prey on my conscience, and likely because the ostracized person was Jewish, and with a "Jewish nose," like me.

What I want to stress, and by way of conclusion, is that acting shamefully and fitting in go hand in hand. And groups and communities are defined by boundaries, and in order for the boundaries to have meaning there have to be people on both sides, in and out, one of "us" and one of "them," friends and enemies, Americans and Un-Americans. And like Jerome Robbins—"like little Jerome Robbins," I find myself wanting to write—we carry the shame with us, casting its shadow on whatever we may be able to accomplish as a result of being part of the group.

I would hardly excuse Robbins for his naming names to the House Committee on Un-American Activities. There were others, including people with less money and status, who refused to testify or who refused to name names. Several ended up in prison, including the scriptwriters Lester Cole and Ring Lardner Jr., who in Danbury Prison joined the former HUAC Chairman, former US Representative J. Parnell Thomas, himself convicted for embezzling federal funds. Those who stood up to the Committee or to the wave of persecution include famous people such as Zero Mostel (later the star of Robbins's *Fiddler on the Roof*), Lillian Hellman, Pete Seeger, Charlie Chaplin, Paul Robeson. But more touching are the unfamiliar names on the various blacklists, people who may have lost more and had less to fall back on when they were ostracized. Selecting at random from a Wikipedia list of "Others first blacklisted after June 1950," I come to Anne Froelick, who began her writing career while serving as secretary to Howard Koch, then a writer for Orson Welles's *The Mercury Theatre on the Air*. Taylor assisted Koch on his adaptation of H.G. Wells's *The War of the Worlds* . . . Taylor was involved in causes such as fighting fascism and promoting unions and desegregation, which reportedly led her to join the Communist Party. In 1951, Taylor's party membership caused her husband, Philip Taylor, to lose his job as a manufacturing planner at Lockheed. She continued to try to make a living as a writer, no longer using the name her parents had given her. She wrote four plays that were produced locally and co-wrote a comic novel, *Press on Regardless*, . . .

This Wikipedia article on the Hollywood blacklist calls attention to John Henry Faulk, host of an afternoon comedy radio show and a leftist active in his union, the American Federation of Television and Radio Artists. He was scrutinized by AWARE, one of the firms that during those years made money (paid for "nice homes," for straightening kids' teeth) by investigating other people's possible communist sympathies or "disloyalty." Marked as unfit, Faulk was fired by CBS Radio. In 1957, by filing a suit against AWARE, he became a leader of the fight to end the blacklist.

Jerome Robbins's testimony before HUAC was his second circumcision, by which he became, in addition to Jewish, fully American. He wanted desperately to fit in, and he did. He fit in better than almost any American of his generation. (And I would like to think that he was able to use his millions and his status to help, in whatever way, the gay movement or individual homosexuals. What I have heard is that he gave a lot of money to the New York Public Library for some kind of dance archive.) What he would also seem to have learned along the way is that there is a price for fitting in. It can be a terrible price.

Excerpts from Robbins's testimony to HUAC

From *Thirty Years of Treason: Excerpts from Hearings Before the House Committee on Un-American Activities, 1938-1968*, selected and edited by Eric Bentley (Thunder's Mouth Press/Nation Books, 1971, 2002).

Committee staff member Frank S. Tavenner: What was the inducement that led you into the Communist Party?

Robbins: The Communist Political Association had been presented to me as an organization which was very much for minorities and for advancing their causes. This interested me very much. I had had, prior to my joining, several instances of very painful moments because of minority prejudice. This was naturally an appeal for me.

Tavenner: Will you give us the names of other persons who were in this group whom you can identify?

Robbins offered six names, after which Committee member Representative Bernard W. Kearney thanked him for his "very frank and unusual testimony," and Committee member Representative Clyde Doyle said, "I want to join in heartily complimenting you on doing what you have done." Doyle told Robbins that some of the people who had been asked to testified had referred to those who named names as "stool pigeons and informers. You realize, no doubt, that when you volunteered the names of other Communists whom you knew to be Communists that you would, by those people at least, be put in that class. . . . What is it in your conscience, or what was it in your experience, that makes you . . . willing to come here, in spite of the fact that you knew some other people . . . would put you down as a stool pigeon, and voluntarily testify as you have today?"

Robbins: I've examined myself. I think I made a great mistake before in entering the Communist Party, and I feel that I am doing the right thing as an American.

V

What Shall I Learn of Parenting or Parenting of Me?

This was my curious labor all summer—to make this portion of the earth's surface, which had yielded only cinquefoil, blackberries, johnswort, and the like, before, sweet wild fruits and pleasant flowers, produce instead this pulse. What shall I learn of beans or beans of me? I cherish them, I hoe them, early and late I have an eye to them; and this is my day's work.

—Henry David Thoreau, *Walden*

19

Of wonders still

At the back of a restaurant a dozen mothers holding their infants to their chests. There is a slight sense of uncertainty, insecurity, such as one may see with first-time mothers. Am I holding my baby correctly? How does my baby compare to these other babies? How do I compare to these other mothers?

Our approach to child-rearing is not very efficient, I think. One or two parents devoted to raising just one child, or at most a few children. And think of all the help these parents need from nannies, babysitters, grandparents, childcare workers, teachers, pediatricians. And how many of these mothers, or their spouses, can be naturally gifted at childcare, or well-trained by their own parents, or well-prepared to learn to be good parents, or well-prepared for juggling the ups and downs of their own lives with the ups and downs of their children's lives? Surely in our modern, high-tech, productivity-oriented society we could devise a better, more efficient system. Indeed we have been making some strides toward developing just such a system, complete with infant formulas and breast pumps and round-the-clock daycare—giving mothers (and fathers) just a few weeks to cuddle and struggle with their children before the parents go back to their jobs and the babies are entrusted to the care of (poorly paid) professionals, some of whom have tons of experience and all of whom are tasked with feeding, keeping clean, entertaining, educating, exercising, putting to sleep several babies at once.

Well, you can see where I am headed with this. Will we come to say that it is a great luxury, both for parents and for children, to be able to raise and be raised one-on-one, or in small family groupings by their own parents? Will this luxury be reserved for some segment of the rich (in purse or spirit)? Will we come to say that our society can no longer afford this luxury? Our economy is not as strong as it once was, or we have other priorities—fighting terrorism? driving large cars? continually updating our electronic equipment? taking care of our elderly citizens? going on cruises and to casinos? Or simply a need to be buying more and more products and services every year—or risk the collapse of our economy, our way of life, our whole system of values?

What will become of children when their care has become completely monetized, off-sited? What will become of parents? A Chinese colleague and I have been exchanging e-mails about the poverty, or poverties, of our social lives in a modern big city where people are too busy getting ahead (and keeping their jobs)—and staying in shape and playing with their cellphones—to have time for what used to be called friendship. By contrast, and luckily, she has her relationship with her two young sons, and I have my relationship with my slightly older son.

Jonah is a big walker, and so, as I reported to Li, he chose for us to walk to the theater this past Sunday—three miles—and to walk back as well. And when we walk is when we talk. I believe that for suburban parents and children the equivalent experience is riding in a car; this is when they talk. A psychologist recently explained to me that children do not feel comfortable talking face to face; walking or riding in a car positions them in such a way that they can talk with ease. I am trying to remember what Jonah and I, this past Sunday, talked about; the only thing that comes to mind is the few minutes of conversation about whether the US government made the right decision in dropping an atom bomb on Hiroshima. That may sound like a gruesome and not very intimate subject, but above all the conversation was a respectful, open-ended exchange of views as we wended our way past the tourists and shoppers on Manhattan's Sixth Avenue.

In leaving the mothers at the back of the restaurant and bicycling home to meet Jonah, make him an early dinner and get him started on his homework, I was reminded of one of my favorite stanzas of poetry, and this notwithstanding that the stanza is a translation from a Russian poem I have never been able to track down, and that the poem, ostensibly, concerns not first-time mothers but rather men such as me.

> Women, make haste to love us,
> For we sing of wonders still,
> And we are the last thin cracks
> That progress has yet to fill!

— Vadim Shershenevich, translator unknown

20

What shall I learn of parenting or parenting of me?

Among the paradoxes of Zen teaching: a central teaching is that you cannot learn from teaching. From a Zen perspective, teaching and all its baggage—e.g. the idea that there are things (practices, ideas) to learn—has nothing to do with enlightenment. Every minute a student spends trying to grasp or master some something that a teacher, or the world, might have to teach is not only a minute without meaning, but a minute whose meaninglessness is likely being resisted. And thus one can be both amused and disturbed by the proliferation of ostensibly Zen (or Chan or Seon) texts that include comments about how study is not the way to enlightenment.

I have been led to set down these words in part because they must also amuse and disturb a writer of intellectual essays who is also a parent. We might say quickly that people who are deeply involved in parenting, and who are thus good parents, have little time for or interest in reading books and articles about the subject. And they may have yet less interest in reading an essay about the lack of usefulness of such books and essays!

I come to all this, or come back to it, after reading a popular magazine article about the contemporary challenge of trying to have a successful career and be a good parent. An implication of the article was that there were right and wrong approaches and that there were policies and programs that might be adopted to make this task easier. The author had given up a high-level job in the US government in order to devote more time to her children, while also returning to full-time university teaching and her active writing career, and while continuing to give about 40 speeches a year at various places around the country or the world. She described one of the rules she had often lived by, which was that dinner time was family time: From 6 to 7:30 p.m. she ate dinner with her family and was not available to attend meetings. (Unless, of course, she was giving a speech in another city or country.) It has not been my experience that one can be much of a parent (mother or father) with this level of commitment.

There is not space here (or in the universe?) to do more than touch on all the possible meanings and implications of a phrase such as "good parenting." For instance, what is the "good" we are trying to achieve? If we are trying to produce a product, a "good adult," what should be the goodness of such a being and why do we call it goodness? And are we producers thinking of our children like cars on assembly lines and trying to avoid "lemons," and . . . ? In the midst of all this I will propose that my experience has led me to place a good deal of faith in the idea that children thrive to the extent that their parents (fathers and mothers) spend a lot of time playing and just being with them, and give them their undivided attention during these times. (No cellphones.) Thus, in my view, travelling around the world giving speeches would not be a way of being a good parent, nor would lying on one's couch re-reading John Blofeld's introduction to his translation *The Zen Teaching of Huang Po* and then turning on the computer to start drafting an essay. (Writing, too, has its assembly-line-like qualities.)

But there is a larger point here. For me reading and writing have been great gifts, great drugs, great pleasures, and for all I can imagine the thrills and engagement of high-level government jobs and of university teaching and of speaking to eager audiences, . . . In a first draft I wrote that such activities pale in comparison to parenting, but this ignored the ecstasy of creation and indeed of many forms of vigorous striving, and no matter how meagre or unsuccessful the results may be. Drawing concentrates the mind in an extraordinary way, and there is a warmth and connectedness in playing music, and there is the enthusiasm of going all out with other people, working on a project, playing on a team, and . . . And yet I would not reject my initial idea of the pallor of such activities when compared to parenting. A central memory: 2, 3 a.m., lying on a cold and drafty floor in a little house in upstate New York, holding Jonah's hand through the bars of his crib—sometimes it would be for an hour or more, and I was not lost to how physically uncomfortable I was, nor to the fact that I wanted nothing more than to stay there—forever, if need be—until Jonah fell back asleep.

Jonah is now 12. The government official/professor's children were in high school. We might say that it is easy for parents during this stage not to be so all-absorbed and often to feel unwanted and in the way. We struggle with letting go as our children struggle with going. It could well be easy to accept an invitation to speak in Singapore, and for some large sum of money, when one's children are looking so pleased by the prospect of having the house to themselves and no one to get up from her or his computer to tell them to turn their own computers off. But my overarching point here is that if we are speaking in a vaguely Buddhist or religious way of higher forms of existence, then—the occasional Picasso excepted—what sense does it make that so many parents give so much more time to policy deliberations, speech making, essay writing, teaching or the arts (or selling shoes or drugs, or writing code, driving a truck, drawing blood) rather than to spending time with their children?

Ironically, even from a policy perspective, it is hard to see the sense in how we allocate our time. Since *The Republic,* at least, we have had an idea that the thriving of a society depends on the moral, intellectual and practical education of the youngest generation, and Freud, Winnicott and many another have helped call our attention to the importance of the care and attention children receive in their first years. But I would make my particular point in another way. It is thought to be "good" for a child if her or his parents have undistracted time to play with and just be with her or him. In my experience it is also "good" for the parent. That is, it can be a lot of fun, and it is engaging on a very deep level. When we "choose"— or, more likely, are forced by economic forces and social pressures, and by our fears of deeper engagements—not to spend time with our children, it is we, the parents, who are losing out.

My mother, who studied child development, used to say that many parents simply do not know how to play with children. And, I would add, many do not know how to converse with small children, except in "baby talk," an invention of rigid adults. Relaxing and just playing—be this with children or with another adult—turns out to be more difficult than we may have imagined. This may explain a number of business trips, weekends spent in offices, and so forth.

The destination of this essay has been to say that there are a fair number of people who already know (in their bones, as it were) that parenting is good for parents. These people are not high-ranking government officials, distinguished university professors or compulsive essay writers. As a result of events, circumstances, fate or any number of choices, large and small, that they have made, they can and do give lots of time and attention to their children. They are people whose primary occupation is parenting. From one perspective they—and perhaps their children as well from some perspectives?—have paid and continue to pay a tremendous price for their having gone into this line of work/play. Unless they are lucky inheritors, these people and their children may not have the social status or money of those who have gone down other paths. (And likely they are missing out on great artistic and intellectual experiences as well!) These people do not write magazine articles or essays or practice Buddhist meditation. Likely they have few hobbies, and such hobbies as they do have are not particularly challenging or awe-inspiring. They do not have stunning gardens or compete in triathlons or play in a quartet. But they may well be closer to living the lives that various experts and philosophizers, myself included, can't stop talking about. I would not propose that these people are enlightened, but if it makes sense to speak of distances in this regard, I would say that these people may be closer to "knowing"—in their bones again—what enlightenment might involve.

One of Thoreau's books is *A Week on the Concord and Merrimack Rivers*. I would pause to note an implication in the "A Week" part of the title: In the midst of the *glandissage*, the farting around, of a human life, we may have a few moments—all told a week or two—of deeper connection. In any case, at one point Thoreau writes of men who have been out every day of their lives; greater men than Homer, or Chaucer, or Shakespeare, only they never got to say so; they never took to the way of writing. Look at their fields, and imagine what they might write, if ever they should put pen to paper. Or what they have not written on the face of the earth already, clearing, and burning, and scratching, and harrowing, and ploughing, and subsoiling, in and in, and out and out, and over and over, again and again, erasing what they had already written for want of parchment.

We might think of this as a polyphonic passage. One voice forms part of Thoreau's repeated critique of economic man, living to produce and accumulate, and thereby not really living at all. Another voice embraces rather than critiques these farmers.

Adding one of my voices to this latter, embracing voice, and now also coming back to the Zen paradox with which I began, I note that the person who has, by whatever lucky accident, found a way or ways of escaping from subject-object duality is not giving classes or writing books. The parent who knows the fruits of parenting is not giving classes or writing books or seeking out high-level jobs. The farmer who is fully farming has no need to save a little time to ask himself or, like Thoreau in *Walden*, to pose as a question for others: "What shall I learn of beans or beans of me?" We might say that the parents who just parent, like the farmers who just farm, have a tendency to be overlooked, and to overlook themselves. And "good" for them.

Afterword

Sometime after I completed this essay I had an opportunity to spend time with a family member who was reaching the end of her life and needed constant care, much of which was provided by home health aides who happened to be immigrants from Uganda. In a sense we in the family were lucky that the dying person had sufficient wealth to be able to pay for good quality, round-the-clock care. And this also allowed us to continue working at our professional jobs and saved us from doing the cleaning and toilet-related work which some of us had done, and had not minded doing, when our children were little.

At the invalid's bedside I was reminded of when my son was very little. It was partly the complete dependency that brought back these memories, but also the fact that the dying person was taking a lot of morphine, had difficulty articulating her thoughts, at times was hallucinating. There were a few days in the midst of this experience—which was, in many ways, a nightmare—there were a few days when I felt that I understood this person's mental processes much as I had once understood the infant Jonah's. It was as if her unconscious spoke directly to my conscious mind; conventional language was not necessary.

During this period I felt envious of the home health aides, particularly of the woman who spent every night half awake in the same room with the dying person, and was thus there to witness the whole process and hear everything the dying person had to say. My professional job paid me about four times more per hour than the aide was being paid, and of course it was a much higher-status job. But it was not nearly so interesting, so directly engaged with and in touch with life (which is to say, with life and death).

It is in many ways more frightening to raise a child than to take care of a dying person. With people who are dying, if you really screw up they die, which is where they were headed in any case. And often the patient has at least some interest in dying sooner rather than later. With children you are helping them prepare for what you and they hope will be many decades of life, with all its challenges most certainly included. It can also be more rewarding to raise a child because if you give the necessary time and attention, and if the child is reasonably healthy to begin with, he or she may well grow stronger, and you may rightly feel that you have played a key role in this growth. Perhaps helping a person die always brings a feeling of failure (along with other, less burdensome feelings). The patient has died, and, although death is a natural consequence of life and may have relieved the patient of physical and psychological suffering, it seems like a failure.

It is also the case that living and working in complex societies, and often working in large, complex organizations as well, we have few opportunities to feel truly effective. At our jobs, if we are fortunate we may be able to accomplish some things that we have wanted to accomplish, and we may be able to see some of these accomplishments last a little while. But even in such fortunate circumstances it may be hard to pinpoint the value of these accomplishments. Supposing, for example, that we have managed to cut costs or raise revenues, or to develop some system that means fewer workers are needed or more detailed information can be collected. Supposing that with great ingenuity we and our colleagues are able to see things on monitors or spreadsheets that human beings have never before seen. There may well be times when one feels that such accomplishments are indeed substantive, and so is wet clay. Helping to raise a child, taking care of a sick or dying person, one has an opportunity to feel effective at quite another level.

My experiences with the dying are much too minimal for me to write a whole essay on this subject, but I propose that, as with parenting, so with caring for the aged: it is a gift to the caretakers as much as to the people who are being taken care of. Most of the other activities of our lives, be they money-seeking or leisure activities, pale in comparison to the richness of helping a person die and being a witness to the process.

I do not believe that writers, or artists more generally, change the world. We are at times servants of larger forces—the interests of capital being one of the largest in these modern times. What a writer can do is to help people perceive somewhat more clearly the lives they are living, the circumstances in which they find themselves, the nature of the forces that are channeling their behavior, their thoughts and dreams included. From this perspective, the present essay takes its place in a certain category of pieces that speak about how larger forces—among them, capital certainly and also our animal instinct to keep trying to increase our physical and psychological security—have twisted our lives, often distancing us from the richest actitivities, the most engaged, that life has to offer.

21

Nurture

There was a time, in a youthful phase, when I was going to Russia for a few weeks each year to work on my Russian, and I would rent a room with a Russian "family" (a woman with perhaps a child or grandchild or two). After my first such visit I had all sorts of theories about Russian families. My second such visit led to a dual realization: not all Russian families were like my first one, and, given this fact, it was also quite possible that there were many other types of Russian families than just these two. It was quite possible I would never know enough Russian families to write intelligently about them. It was from a similar perspective, I believe, that someone wisely said that you should never write about a place you had been in for more than two weeks or less than two years. And we are also back to one of my favorite insights of Greek mathematics: the oneness of the one (of the first Russian family, in our case) is negated by the existence of the two (the second family), which in turn makes way for a world of possibility: the three, four, five and so forth, towards infinity.

I have begun with this sort of disclaimer above all to try not to fly too close to the sun in making the following observations of one writer (me) with, as it were, one houseplant and one child. The child's name is Jonah. Another kind of writer or gardener would also know the plant's species or common name. I picked it up more than a year ago in the garbage area of my apartment building. It was mangy, half dead. We might wonder about the circumstances and feelings surrounding its abandonment. Had one of my neighbors tried for quite some time to get this plant to flourish and given up in frustration? ("Clearly *my* thumbs are not green!") Were adult children cleaning out a deceased parent's apartment? Had the plant been an unwanted gift, or spoiled when a young child tried peeing in the pot? Did the person who left the plant in that garbage area have a moment of feeling, conscious or unconscious, that s/he was abandoning a living thing? There are times when we abandon (or "throw out") inanimate objects—an old tape player, a book we have never read, a child's baseball glove—and feel the ache of separation, a shadow of mortality. (And the traumas of birth, weaning, going off to college?)

At first, notwithstanding the plant's superficial ugliness, manginess, I hung the pot on the rod over my bath, on the shower-curtain rod. I never did any pruning. I'm not a pruner, though I am a repotter, and at some point I repotted the plant, with positive effect. Then, a few months ago, I transferred it to the window ledge, by the little frosted window above the bathtub. There it received a little more direct sunlight and began to flourish. It flourished so vigorously that I had to move it to one of my bedroom windows where now it is as green and unmangy as green and unmangy could be.

Plants usually respond like this to my care, as to many another person's. I doubt that our green-thumbedness is based on any great talents or secret knowledge. In my case, above all I am a careful waterer. I wait until the soil is dry to the touch and then I water the plant thoroughly until water fills the saucer below. And if a plant is not thriving I try a little fertilizer or move the plant to a different location. I remove yellowing leaves, and in the winter when the heating system dries out the air I occasionally spray the leaves with water.

I also like to think that I have had similar success with a seemingly more complex plant: Jonah. And perhaps my technique has been similar. I have spent a lot of time with him. I have roughhoused and played ball with him and coached his teams and read to him and next to him and watched TV with him. I bathed with him when he was little and held his hand as we walked around town. I give him a hug and kiss most every morning and night and take walks and talk with him when things are not going right. In the evenings I have not used babysitters, but have put him to bed myself. I try not to keep him up too late, even when we are having a good time together. If there seem to be problems at school, I go to see teachers and have frank talks with Jonah. I speak up (and write way too many, too lengthy e-mails—not one of my better habits). On a few occasions when there have seemed to be problems we could not understand or did not know how to deal with, Jonah's mother and I have gone to a child psychologist for advice.

I am here taking all this to be a kind of watering, or of a combination of waiting and watching for dryness and watering thoroughly when watering seems needed. I note that I have vastly oversimplified the past 14 wonderful, but hardly always wonderful or happy years. Among other things, I have for present purposes largely written out of the story Jonah's very involved mother and also the fact that she has long lived in a separate apartment, sharing custody of *our* son. And it would be obnoxious and pointless for me, the father, to detail Jonah's accomplishments and shortfalls to date or to quote the best and worst lines from his (not wonderful) report cards. And I have long had the sense that adolescence is not going to respond so simply and productively to my simple, if time- and attention-demanding technique. Interestingly, two of my plants have grown too large to fit happily in the sunnier spots of my house, and life for them, and thus for me watching and trying to help them, has become more difficult. As Jonah, growing rapidly, struggles for an impossible though much ballyhooed independence and autonomy, while also missing the warmth and security of his first months and years, and as his mother and I, though proud to see him becoming a man and making his way in the world, must also feel, like a cloth tearing, beloved bonds being rent, . . . How can this be easy? We must grow up as fast as our son, and learn the lesson that so many parents these days are finding it hard to learn: how to leave our child alone, how to re-make full lives for ourselves after Jonah's own full life will have taken him some distance away from us.

Meanwhile, for the past many years Jonah has been flourishing like a many leaved, young green plant. And, oddly enough, I, while raising Jonah and tending my plants, have written hundreds upon hundreds of pages about human ignorance and about how we cannot know who we are and what the consequences of our actions are and what we should do. And about how we often do not want to know, or do not "really" want to know. And about how, in any case, knowledge cannot save us from mortality or from other aspects of the human predicament. Sometimes—increasingly—this work has seemed a hair off to me, a significant hair off. In the sense that the work seems to ignore, to deliberately ignore, some very basic things that I do know. If only about caring for houseplants and raising one particular child.

Watering my plants the other day I had a thought about the nature-nurture debate that philosophers and others have long engaged in. The view from my apartment has been all on the nurture side. It may be the case that many people—many busy, overworked or otherwise engaged parents, along with various pundits, politicians and business leaders—may wish to deny this view of childrearing. That is, for personal, political or economic reasons people may wish to insist that a child's genes or in-born character count for most everything, and thus when a child has problems at school or with the police, the parents may assign him (or her) to a psychologist, a professional who should know how to help the child deal with *his* problems.

But again, the view from my apartment has been all on the nurture side. (Which is also to say that I rarely see children as having their own problems; these are family problems, school problems, societal problems.) Often in times of trouble—wilting, leaves turning brown—it is enough to keep watering with more scrupulous regularity, but not excessively, and a plant will, as it were, revive on its own. And similarly with Jonah and regular meals, regular bedtimes, more time with him mom or dad.

I n studying and reflecting on the work of great philosophers and other intellectuals, and in studying the history of societies and of individuals around me, I have learned (rightly or wrongly?) that we cannot know what the good is, and there is no meaning to or purpose of life, and so on and so forth. In recent decades some philosophers have decided that the good is "flourishing." In my experience, this has above all simply shifted the definitional problem from one set of letters ("the good") to another ("flourishing"). What is the right or best or a good way to live or be? Unanswerable questions, and unavoidable ones. It is easy enough to observe that some of the most superficially successful people—prominent entrepreneurs and Wall Street players, Nobel Prize winners, performers and athletes, famous writers—are in many ways limited human beings, driven often by demons or false gods, or by what might be called existential panic, or by insecurities deeply rooted in their childhoods. These are plants that take up a good deal of space and light, and may block light that might have nurtured others. Do we want to refer to this phenomenon or to some of these people as flourishing?

"Why am I so byoo-ti-full?" I will always remember overhearing Jonah singing that line in the bath when he was something like 4 years old. "Flourishing" (as I am calling it) has not led him to be extraordinarily creative, to get the best marks at school, to be notably helpful to others, to be surrounded by friends, etc. It has to do rather with self-confidence (and thus to a talent for acting and public speaking) and with contentment and engagement with his particular life, his rooms, his activities, his parents; a pleasure at having time by himself and a pleasure in playing with others, competing and making up skits and games together. He knows what he likes and does not like, has a quite sophisticated understanding of life and plenty of good jokes. Touch wood, may such flourishing last, and may it survive, his entry into the work world. (It is not insignificant that Jonah is growing up in the United States where children are coddled, told how great they and their ideas and their soccer kicks and drawings are. For better and worse, this approach takes—or, rather, appears to take—much of the work out of childhood.)

I would not ignore the role of social and economic factors, and this essay may lend its weight (however light) to arguments for policies that would help poor (and rich) parents spend more time with their children. But the essay remains fundamentally a middle-class piece: written by a middle-class parent with a middle-class child, and for middle-class readers. And I would note, too, that Jonah has the good fortune of having two parents who earn their livings in the bureaucracy, who earn decent salaries (with health insurance and defined-benefit pensions) without having to work monstrously long days. Between his mother and I we have twelve weeks of vacation and twelve "personal days" a year to spend with Jonah. Two afternoons a week I work from home so that I can be there to meet him after school, give him a kiss and some food and point him in the direction of his homework. We are not rich and have no "nice things" (no car, no big TV, no doorman, no country house), but economically, at least for the time being, we really have everything we need. When Jonah's shoes get too small or he loses a school book, we buy replacements. We take taxis, and when (as often happens) I am too tired to cook or want to get out of our 800 sq. ft. apartment, we go out to eat.

Someone who, thanks to luck or talent, gives some evidence of having a green thumb need not go into the landscaping business or join the lecture circuit. And, even at the risk of contradicting what I have written heretofore, I must note that, inevitably, if Anne (Jonah's mother) and I were notably richer or poorer, or if we had had a different child—a girl, for instance—this essay would not be quite the same. At the very least, its idea of flourishing might be somewhat different. But still, I would insist again and again that if a plant or a child receives basic nurturing in a consistent fashion, its, her or his flourishing may be quite appreciable and satisfying, and to the plant or child first and foremost.

22

The connection between shoe-tying and world peace

Allow me to begin with a few notes:

1 Jonah says that in the piece below I got the quote wrong. What he said was, "You think that *if you tied everyone's shoes for them*, there'd be no more war." I suspect that in this case, as in many others, he's right.

2 Subsequently to the conversation recorded here, Jonah developed foot problems, as he has every year because he doesn't tie his shoes correctly—until he develops foot problems and lets me tie his shoes for him.

3 I suppose I should not be surprised that, when I Google, I get more than 1 million hits for "John Wooden shoe tying." These include a YouTube video of an elderly Wooden teaching a boy exactly Jonah's age to tie his shoes. The video also includes one of Wooden's most famous players, Bill Walton, telling about the shock that he and other new players felt when the first thing Wooden did was sit them down and teach them how to put on their shoes and socks. Doing this properly, Walton has said, was the initial lesson for "everything we would need to know for the rest of our lives."

These notes were provoked by a not-untypical parent-walking-child-to-school conversation. I noticed that Jonah's heels were swimming in all the space at the back of his new soccer shoes. I asked if the shoes were too big. No, he said, in fact they were quite comfortable.

"After I tie them," I said, "they're going to be a lot more snug."

"You think," he answered, in my recollection, "that if everyone tied their shoes your way there'd be no more war."

Yes, I thought to myself, he's absolutely right, and not only about me but about morality and moralists more generally. To get one thing right, we think, is to get everything right. Or, more often, it is: To get one thing wrong—have sex out of wedlock or without a condom, tell a lie, litter—is to get everything wrong. And this is also a sign of how misguided the moralists' (we moralists') approach is. Not only is it possible to be wrong in some domains or at some moments and right at others (presuming we have a way of distinguishing right from wrong!), but there is also more than one "right" way to tie one's shoes, or to relate to other human beings, live a life. And it may turn out that my ways are wrong, or that they are right in one context (playing competitive soccer) and wrong in another (making the scene in middle school). If the devil is in the details, it is also the case that one can miss the forest for the trees..

That said, I note that the famous and often triumphant college basketball coach John Wooden is said to have begun each season by teaching his new recruits how to tie their shoes. After dominating game after game on rough-and-tumble urban playgrounds and in steamy high-school gyms, these boys had been wined and dined and promised fame and fortune if only they came to play at UCLA. Then, when they showed up, the coach told them they didn't know how to tie their shoes. Because John Wooden knew not only that well-supported ankles are essential to succeeding and surviving as a basketball player, but also that—I was going to say that he knew that if you get one thing right you get everything right. Or was his primary goal infantilizing his new recruits, firmly establishing himself as the father figure?

Or could it be that the way to get the larger things right (the way to win basketball games? to make it to the NBA? or . . . ?) is to begin by getting the little things right. If we would all just tie our shoes correctly, and put our cellphones away when we were with other people, and make time to give our kids and our parents a kiss before bedtime, . . . There'd be no more war.

"Yeah, right," Jonah would say.

William Eaton has been an award-winning journalist and essayist, a novelist and writer of intellectual dialogues. His "The Professor of Ignorance Condemns the Airplane," was staged in New York in 2014. He is the Executive Editor of *Zeteo: Reading, Looking, Listening . . . Questioning.* His Montaigbakhtinian blog is followed by more than a thousand readers worldwide.
Photo by Sarah Shatz

CPSIA information can be obtained
at www.ICGtesting.com
Printed in the USA
LVOW12s1613180916
505136LV00007B/344/P